CAMBRIDGE NATIONAL LEVEL

Child Development

Revision Guide and Workbook

Renata Paradowska

University Printing House, Cambridge CB2 8BS, United Kingdom

One Liberty Plaza, 20th Floor, New York, NY 10006, USA

477 Williamstown Road, Port Melbourne, VIC 3207, Australia

314–321, 3rd Floor, Plot 3, Splendor Forum, Jasola District Centre, New Delhi – 110025, India

103 Penang Road, #05–06/07, Visioncrest Commercial, Singapore 23846

Cambridge University Press is part of the University of Cambridge.

It furthers the University's mission by disseminating knowledge in the pursuit of education, learning and research at the highest international levels of excellence.

www.cambridge.org
Information on this title: www.cambridge.org/9781009129145

First published 2022

20 19 18 17 16 15 14 13 12 11 10 9 8 7 6 5 4 3 2 1

Printed in Poland by Opolgraf

A catalogue record for this publication is available from the British Library

ISBN 978-1-009-12914-5 Paperback with Digital Access (2 Year)
ISBN 978-1-009-12574-1 Digital Revision Guide and Workbook (2 Years)
ISBN 978-1-009-12575-8 Site License (1 Year)

Additional resources for this publication at www.cambridge.org/9781009129145

Contents

Preparing for the exam

Your Revision Guide and Workbook

This Revision Guide will support you in preparing for the exam for Unit R057 Health and well-being for child development. This is the externally assessed unit of your Child Development J809 course.

The Revision Guide contains two types of pages as shown below:

- Content pages help you revise the content you need to know.
- Workbook pages with practice exam-style questions help you prepare for your exam.

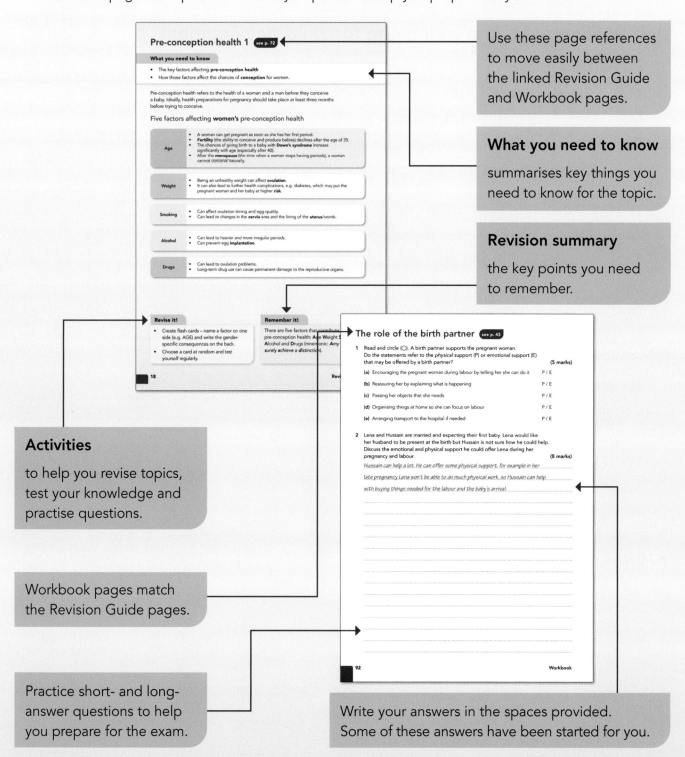

Use these page references to move easily between the linked Revision Guide and Workbook pages.

What you need to know

summarises key things you need to know for the topic.

Revision summary

the key points you need to remember.

Activities

to help you revise topics, test your knowledge and practise questions.

Workbook pages match the Revision Guide pages.

Practice short- and long-answer questions to help you prepare for the exam.

Write your answers in the spaces provided. Some of these answers have been started for you.

Planning your revision

Countdown to the exam

Revision checklists are a good way for you to plan and structure your revision.
They also allow you to make sure you have covered everything you need to cover:

Revision planner checklist

Time before the exam	Things to do	
6–8 weeks	• Draw up a revision timetable so that you know how much time you have to get through everything.	☐
	• Use the revision checklist on page 16 to work out which topics you need to cover.	☐
	• Use the topic area headings and bullets to organise your notes and to make sure you've covered everything in the specification.	☐
	• Don't do too much in one day – a couple of hours of good-quality work in a day is better than trying to cram.	☐
4–6 weeks	• Work out which of the areas you still find difficult and plan when you'll cover them.	☐
	• You may be able to discuss tricky topics with your teacher or class colleagues.	☐
	• As you feel you've got to grips with some of the knowledge, you can 'tick off' the parts that have been worrying you.	☐
	• Make the most of the revision sessions you're offered in class. Don't skip them!	☐
1 week	• Make a daily plan to revise those few topics you're not happy with and look back at your revision cards if you've made some.	☐
Day before	• Try not to cram today – get some exercise and relax in the afternoon.	☐
	• Make sure you know what time and where the exam is and put all your things out (pencils, pens, calculator, bus pass, water) ready for the next day.	☐
	• Get a good night's sleep!	☐

Revise it!

Using the example above, create your own revision checklist. Identify areas that you are not so confident about and think of ways to tackle these.

Revision tips

Choose the methods that work for you

For example:

- use highlighters for key words and phrases
- make note cards
- use mnemonics (the first letter of words): for example, *Amy Will Surely Achieve a Distinction* stands for **A**ge **W**eight **S**moking **A**lcohol and **D**rugs.

Plan your revision

Make a list of all the key dates from when you start your revision up to the exam date.

Don't cram!

Plan to space your revision out so that you don't do everything at once!

Take breaks

Plan regular breaks in your revision. Go for a short walk or get some fresh air. It will make you more focused when you do revise!

Learn everything!

Questions can be asked about **any area** of the specification.

It is easier to answer a question if you have revised everything.

Identify your strengths and weaknesses

Complete the 'Revision checklist' at the end of each chapter and identify areas that you feel less confident about. Allow additional time to revise these areas.

Stay healthy!

Exercise, fresh air, good food and staying hydrated all help your revision.

Variety is the spice of life!

Mix up your revision methods. Watch videos and listen to podcasts as well as making notes and mind maps.

Practise!

Practising exam-style questions will help you get to grips with the question types, time pressure and format of the exam.

Attend revision classes!

Don't skip revision classes – it can really help to revise with your friends as well as by yourself.

Use mind maps!

Mind maps are great for connecting ideas and memorising information more easily and quickly.

Find a quiet space

It can be difficult to revise in loud or busy spaces, so try to find somewhere calm to work. You could use headphones and music to block out distractions.

Revision techniques

Flash cards/revision cards

These are useful for summarising content, key word definitions and important facts. Use colours to make certain things stand out – for example, you could use different colours for advantages and disadvantages or for key words. You can test yourself using the revision cards.

Mind maps

These are a really useful visual summary of information and you can put them on the wall. They allow you to show links between ideas and concepts. You can start by adding the topic to the centre of the diagram and then add the sub-topics around that and a summary of the information.

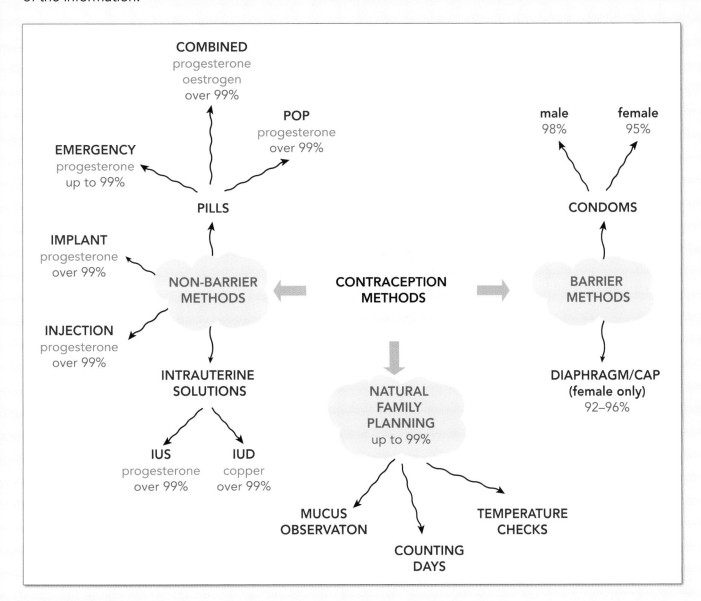

Revise it!

Create a mind map for a topic of your choice.

Highlighting

Making notes and highlighting key areas to go back to is a good way of working out what you know and don't know. You can then use these notes as you come to your final revision. You can use different colours to highlight different factors or different types of information. For example, any key medical terminology could be in yellow.

Summaries

On the revision pages of this book, you'll find summaries of key ideas and themes. Use these to help you summarise the key points you'll need to remember to answer questions on those topics. For example, you need to know factors affecting pre-conception health. You can make a summary of these yourself – and if you think through these points in the exam, you are more likely to remember them.

Mnemonics

A **mnemonic** is another useful way of remembering key facts by using the first letter of each of the parts to make up a memorable phrase. For example, in case of pre-conception health: **A**ge **W**eight **S**moking **A**lcohol and **D**rugs (mnemonic: **Amy will surely achieve a distinction**).

Quizzes

Many people enjoy quizzes, and creating and sharing quizzes with your friends and class is a great way to remember facts and concepts. You could suggest to your teacher that, in pairs, you create a quiz of ten questions each week and go through with another pair – swapping answers. It's also a good way for you to check your knowledge. Make a note of the areas where you really didn't know the answer and add these to your revision list.

Practice questions

Doing past papers and practice exam questions is an essential part of your revision. It prepares you for answering different types of exam questions and allows you to become familiar with the wording of the questions used by OCR. For example, the command word *state* requires a different approach than *discuss*. See page 120 for the full list of command words used on the exam.

You should also use the mark scheme. This will help you understand how to get full marks for each question.

It is helpful to highlight key words in exam questions so you're clear what the question is asking before you answer it.

Getting ready for the exam

Use the revision checklist and all your revision material to make sure you are as prepared as possible; practise plenty with exam questions and quick quizzes.

In the exam

Give yourself time to complete the whole paper, and check through it for mistakes. Most importantly, try to stay calm and relaxed – remember, this is your time to show off what you know!

Get plenty of sleep

Make sure you get a good night's sleep the night before the exam. Don't stay up late cramming as you need time to switch off and relax before going to bed.

Keep hydrated but don't drink too much

It's important that you stay hydrated, but don't overdo it or else you'll be running to the toilet. Exams can make you a bit nervous too which means you might need to go to the toilet a bit more frequently. Water is best.

Eat a good, healthy meal

Have a good, healthy meal that you enjoy the night before the exam and a filling breakfast on the day of the exam to give you a boost ready for your exam.

Make sure you have all the things you need

Get everything ready the night before – including all writing equipment, a calculator if you need one (and are allowed one), a water bottle, tissues if you have a sniff, and any identification you might need (candidate number if you have been given one).

Getting ready for the exam

Set your alarm

If your exam is in the morning, set an alarm or two so you have plenty of time to get to the exam. If you're still worried about oversleeping, ask a friend or someone in your family to make sure you're up.

Arrive in plenty of time

Know when and where the exam is. Get there at least 15 minutes before it starts. If your exam is in an unfamiliar part of the school and away from where you normally study, you might have to leave home a bit earlier. Don't be distracted on the way!

Don't be tempted to do too much cramming

Too much last-minute cramming can scramble your brain! You may find that being relaxed will help you recall the facts you need rather than attempting last-minute cramming, but you may also want to revise the key facts before setting off for the exam.

What to expect in the exam

As part of your qualification in Child Development you will be taking an exam that is worth 40 percent of your marks. It is important that from the beginning you start to think about the exam and the skills you'll need to get the best possible grade. Answering exam questions is a skill. Like any other skill, it can be learnt, practised and improved.

Below is an outline of what to expect in the exam, the types of questions and what the paper looks like. You need to answer **all** the questions.

Types of questions to expect in the exam

Exam questions can be asked about any area of the specification, which means that you have to learn everything!

The exam paper will contain three types of question.

Question type	Description
Short-answer question	• Usually require a one-word answer or a simple sentence. • These could be multiple choice, where you select a correct answer from a list of possibilities. • Worth 1–2 marks.
Medium-answer question	• Usually require an answer of 3 or 4 sentences. • Worth 3–6 marks.
Long-answer question	• Open response question where you are expected to do a piece of extended writing. • Worth up to 8 marks. • These questions allow you to be assessed on the quality of your written communication.

Understanding the language of the exam

The command word is the key term that tells you how to answer the question. It is essential to know what the different command words mean and what they are asking you to do. It is easy to confuse the words and provide too much information, not enough information or the wrong information. The tables below will help you understand what each command word is asking you to do.

Command words that ask you to get creative

Command word	OCR definition	How you should approach it
Create	• Produce a visual solution to a problem (for example: a mind map, flow chart or visualisation).	Show your answer in a visual way. You might want to use a mind map, flow chart or a diagram. Think about what is the best way to show the required information.
Draw	• Produce a picture or diagram.	Create a picture/diagram to show the relevant information.

Command words that ask you to do your maths

Command word	OCR definition	How you should approach it
Calculate	• Get a numerical answer showing how it has been worked out.	Do your maths. Give the final answer but make sure you show how you got there.

Command words that ask you to choose the correct answer

Command word	OCR definition	How you should approach it
Choose	• Select an answer from options given.	Pick the option that you think is correct.
Circle	• Select an answer from options given.	Draw a circle around the right answer.
Identify	• Select an answer from options given. • Recognise, name or provide factors or features.	Either choose the correct answer from those given or write the name, factors or features that are asked for.

Command words that ask you to add to something

Command word	OCR definition	How you should approach it
Annotate	• Add information, for example to a table, diagram or graph, until it is final. • Add all the needed or appropriate parts.	Add short notes to the table/diagram/graph to say what each part is.
Complete	• Add all the needed or appropriate parts. • Add information, for example to a table, diagram or graph, until it is final.	Add the information that is missing. Often you will need to give just one word as an answer but sometimes you may need to write more. You may need to finish drawing a diagram or graph.
Fill in	• Add all the needed or appropriate parts. • Add information, for example to a table, diagram or graph, until it is final.	Add the information that is missing. Often you will need to give just one word as an answer but sometimes you may need to write more.
Label	• Add information, for example to a table, diagram or graph, until it is final. • Add all the necessary or appropriate parts.	This often refers to a diagram or a picture. Add words or short phrases to say what each part is. You could add arrows next to your label that point to the right part of the diagram/graph.

Command words that ask you to give the main points

Command word	OCR definition	How you should approach it
Outline	• Give a short account, summary or description.	Write about the main points. Don't write lots of detailed information.
State	• Give factors or features. • Give short, factual answers.	Give a short answer that names factors or features of something. Sometimes you will be asked to give a certain number of factors/features.

Command words that ask you to be factual

Command word	OCR definition	How you should approach it
Describe	• Give an account including all the relevant characteristics, qualities or events. • Give a detailed account of.	This is the 'what'. Write about **what** something is.
Explain	• Give reasons for and/or causes of. • Use the words 'because' or 'therefore' in answers.	This is the 'how' and/or the 'why'. Write about **how** something happens or works and **why** it does.

Command words that ask you to give an opinion

Command word	OCR definition	How you should approach it
Analyse	• Separate or break down information into parts and identify its characteristics or elements. • Explain the pros and cons of a topic or argument and make reasoned comments. • Explain the impacts of actions using a logical chain of reasoning.	This term wants you to write about the details. Write about each part in turn, giving key information and saying what is good or bad about it.
Compare and contrast	• Give an account of the similarities and differences between two or more items or situations.	'Compare' means to say what is the *same* about two (or more) things. 'Contrast' means to say what is *different* about two (or more) things.
Discuss	• Present, analyse and evaluate relevant points (for example, for/against an argument).	Write about something in detail, including its strengths and weaknesses. Say what you think about each side of the argument. You don't need to take a side.
Evaluate	• Make a reasoned qualitative judgement considering different factors and using available knowledge/experience.	Write down the arguments for and against something. Then give your opinion about which is the stronger argument.
Justify	• Give good reasons for offering an opinion or reaching a conclusion.	Write what you think would be the best option and say why you think this. Give evidence to support your answer.

Practise it!

Now go to www.cambridge.org/go and complete the practice questions on understanding the exam command words.

Common exam mistakes

Common mistakes	Why it matters!	Solutions
Not attempting a question	You won't get any marks for a blank answer.	• Answer every question. • Write something – you may pick up a few marks, which can add up to make the difference between grades. • Use your general knowledge. • State the obvious. • Think 'What would my teacher say to that?'.
Not answering the question that is asked	You won't get any marks for writing about another topic or for answering the wrong command word.	• Know what the command words are looking for. • RTQ – read the question. • ATQ – answer the question.
Not providing enough points to achieve the marks	You won't gain full marks if you haven't expanded on your answer.	• Look at the number of marks next to the question – one mark = one point; two marks = two points, three marks = three points, etc. • Consider if the question requires further explanation or discussion.

Preparing for the exam

Continued

Common mistakes	Why it matters!	Solutions
Focusing on a single word rather than the whole question	You won't get marks if the question asked you for a specific application that you confused.	• Think twice if the question asks you for a specific application (e.g. benefits for the mother rather than benefits for the child). • Only answer what you are asked about.
Providing multiple answers rather than one firm choice or repeating the same choice in different words	If you provide two to three options to the examiner, and one of them is wrong, you may lose the marks. If you repeat the same thing in different words, you can only be marked once for that answer.	• Decide on one point that you will use. • Consider if your second answer is showing a different point to what has been said before.

Answering long-answer questions

Planning your answer

To help you organise your thoughts it is helpful to plan your answer for 8-mark questions. You don't need to take too long. A spider diagram, for example, will help you get your answer in the right order and it makes sure you don't forget anything. Here is an exemplar spider diagram for the question: 'Discuss the emotional and physical support a partner can offer during pregnancy and labour':

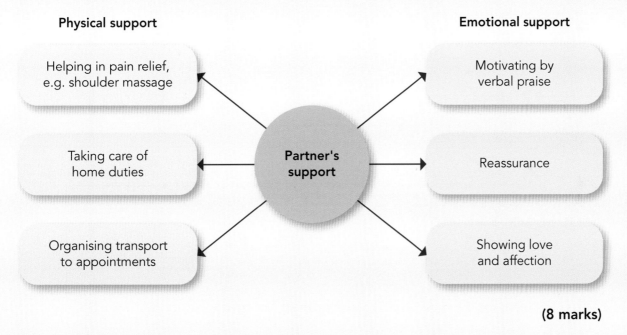

Physical support

Emotional support

Helping in pain relief, e.g. shoulder massage

Taking care of home duties

Organising transport to appointments

Partner's support

Motivating by verbal praise

Reassurance

Showing love and affection

(8 marks)

You don't need to write all of the above. Once you have planned possible points, you can decide if you want to include all of them or perhaps focus on the key three–four aspects and discuss them in more detail. Balance of points and quality of writing is what matters in extended writing questions.

Revise it!

Create a spider diagram plan like the one above for the following question:

'Mackenzie and Heidi care for their ill grandson, Leo. Discuss how carers can meet the social and emotional needs of an ill child.' (8 marks)

Tip: You could refer to page 67 of the Revision Guide to help you.

The exam paper

Make sure you know how long you have got.

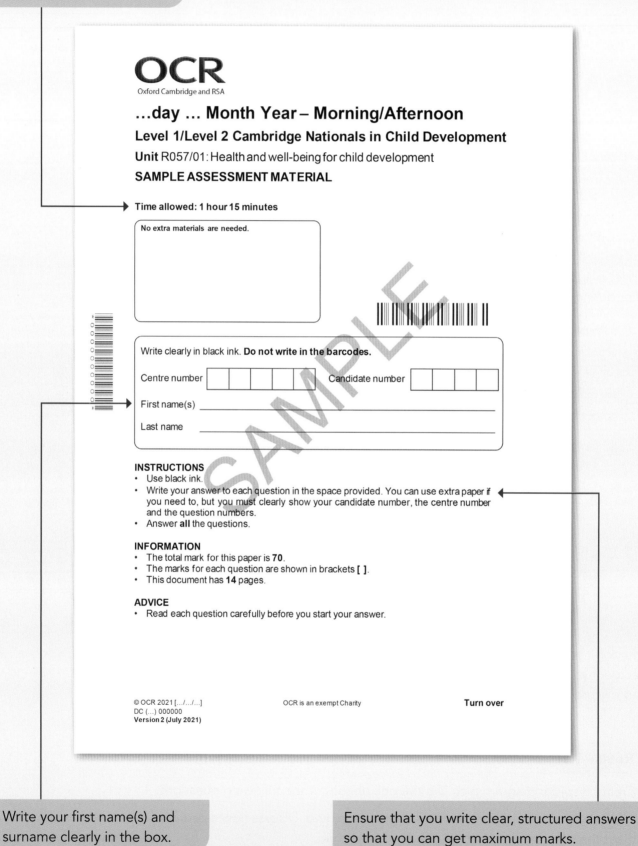

OCR
Oxford Cambridge and RSA

...day ... Month Year – Morning/Afternoon

Level 1/Level 2 Cambridge Nationals in Child Development

Unit R057/01: Health and well-being for child development

SAMPLE ASSESSMENT MATERIAL

Time allowed: 1 hour 15 minutes

No extra materials are needed.

Write clearly in black ink. **Do not write in the barcodes.**

Centre number ☐☐☐☐☐   Candidate number ☐☐☐☐

First name(s) _____

Last name _____

INSTRUCTIONS
- Use black ink.
- Write your answer to each question in the space provided. You can use extra paper if you need to, but you must clearly show your candidate number, the centre number and the question numbers.
- Answer **all** the questions.

INFORMATION
- The total mark for this paper is **70**.
- The marks for each question are shown in brackets **[ ]**.
- This document has **14** pages.

ADVICE
- Read each question carefully before you start your answer.

© OCR 2021 [.../.../...]
DC (...) 000000
Version 2 (July 2021)

OCR is an exempt Charity

Turn over

Write your first name(s) and surname clearly in the box.

Ensure that you write clear, structured answers so that you can get maximum marks.

Highlight or underline key words in the question. Here you need to explain **two** reasons for the blood test at the first antenatal appointment.

2

Section A

1   Anika is pregnant and has her first appointment at the antenatal clinic.

   (a)   State the meaning of **antenatal**.

   ....[1]

   (b)   At the appointment Anika meets some of the health professionals who will support her through her pregnancy.

   Identify **one** health professional who will support Anika through her pregnancy.

   ....[1]

   (c)   One of the routine checks Anika has at her first antenatal appointment is a blood test.

   (i) Explain **two** reasons for this blood test.

   1 ....

   ....

   ....

   2 ....

   ....

   ....

   [4]

   (ii) Identify **three** routine checks or tests, other than a blood test, that are done at an antenatal clinic.

   1 ....

   2 ....

   3 ....

   [3]

Look at the command word in the question. What is it asking you to do?

There are four marks to be gained, so each of the two reasons must be explained enough to get two marks each.

Revision checklist

Topic Area	What you should know			
Topic Area 1: Pre-conception health and reproduction	1.1 Factors affecting pre-conception health for women and men			
	• Pre-conception health 1	☐	☐	☐
	• Pre-conception health 2	☐	☐	☐
	1.2 Other factors affecting pre-conception health for women			
	• Folic acid and immunisations	☐	☐	☐
	1.3 Types of contraception methods and their advantages and disadvantages			
	• Barrier methods of contraception	☐	☐	☐
	• Non-barrier methods of contraception 1	☐	☐	☐
	• Non-barrier methods of contraception 2	☐	☐	☐
	• Natural family planning	☐	☐	☐
	1.4 The structure and function of the reproductive systems			
	• Female reproductive system 1	☐	☐	☐
	• Female reproductive system 2	☐	☐	☐
	• Male reproductive system	☐	☐	☐
	1.5 How reproduction takes place			
	• How reproduction takes place 1	☐	☐	☐
	• How reproduction takes place 2	☐	☐	☐
	• Development of the embryo and foetus	☐	☐	☐
	• Multiple pregnancies	☐	☐	☐
	1.6 The signs and symptoms of pregnancy			
	• Signs and symptoms of pregnancy	☐	☐	☐
Topic Area 2: Antenatal care and preparation for birth	2.1 The purpose and importance of antenatal clinics			
	• Professionals involved in antenatal care	☐	☐	☐
	• Antenatal clinic appointments 1	☐	☐	☐
	• Antenatal clinic appointments 2	☐	☐	☐

2.2 Screening and diagnostic tests			
• Screening tests	☐	☐	☐
• Diagnostic tests	☐	☐	☐
2.3 The purpose and importance of antenatal (parenting) classes			
• Antenatal (parenting) classes 1	☐	☐	☐
• Antenatal (parenting) classes 2	☐	☐	☐
• Antenatal (parenting) classes 3	☐	☐	☐
2.4 The choices available for delivery			
• Choices available for delivery: hospital birth	☐	☐	☐
• Choices available for delivery: home birth	☐	☐	☐
2.5 The role of the birth partner in supporting the mother through pregnancy and birth			
• The role of the birth partner	☐	☐	☐
2.6 The methods of pain relief when in labour			
• Pain relief in labour 1	☐	☐	☐
• Pain relief in labour 2	☐	☐	☐
2.7 The signs that labour has started			
• Signs that labour has started	☐	☐	☐
2.8 The three stages of labour and their physiological changes			
• Stages of labour	☐	☐	☐
2.9 The methods of assisted birth			
• Assisted birth 1	☐	☐	☐
• Assisted birth 2	☐	☐	☐

Topic Area 3: Postnatal checks, postnatal care and the conditions for development	3.1 Postnatal checks			
	• Immediate postnatal checks 1	☐	☐	☐
	• Immediate postnatal checks 2	☐	☐	☐
	• Additional postnatal examinations 1	☐	☐	☐
	• Additional postnatal examinations 2	☐	☐	☐
	3.2 Postnatal care of the mother and baby			
	• Postnatal care 1	☐	☐	☐
	• Postnatal care 2	☐	☐	☐
	3.3 The developmental needs of children from birth to five years			
	• Developmental needs 1	☐	☐	☐
	• Developmental needs 2	☐	☐	☐
	• Developmental needs 3	☐	☐	☐
	• Developmental needs 4	☐	☐	☐
Topic Area 4: Childhood illnesses and a child-safe environment	4.1 Recognise general signs and symptoms of illness in children			
	• Childhood illnesses 1	☐	☐	☐
	• Childhood illnesses 2	☐	☐	☐
	• Childhood illnesses 3	☐	☐	☐
	• Childhood illnesses 4	☐	☐	☐
	• Emergency medical help	☐	☐	☐
	4.2 How to meet the needs of an ill child			
	• Meeting the needs of an ill child 1	☐	☐	☐
	• Meeting the needs of an ill child 2	☐	☐	☐
	• Meeting the needs of an ill child 3	☐	☐	☐

4.3 How to ensure a child-friendly safe environment			
• Hazard prevention 1	☐	☐	☐
• Hazard prevention 2	☐	☐	☐
• Hazard prevention 3	☐	☐	☐
• Safety labels	☐	☐	☐

Pre-conception health 1 see p. 74

What you need to know

- The key factors affecting **pre-conception health**
- How those factors affect the chances of **conception** for women.

Pre-conception health refers to the health of a woman and a man before they conceive a baby. Ideally, health preparations for pregnancy should take place at least three months before trying to conceive.

Five factors affecting **women's** pre-conception health

Age	<ul><li>A woman can get pregnant as soon as she has her first period.</li><li>**Fertility** (the ability to conceive and produce babies) declines after the age of 35.</li><li>The chances of giving birth to a baby with **Down's syndrome** increase significantly with age (especially after 40).</li><li>After the **menopause** (the time when a woman stops having periods), a woman cannot conceive naturally.</li></ul>
Weight	<ul><li>Being an unhealthy weight can affect **ovulation**.</li><li>It can also lead to further health complications, e.g. diabetes, which may put the pregnant woman and her baby at higher **risk**.</li></ul>
Smoking	<ul><li>Can affect ovulation timing and egg quality.</li><li>Can lead to changes in the **cervix** area and the lining of the **uterus/womb**.</li></ul>
Alcohol	<ul><li>Can lead to heavier and more irregular periods.</li><li>Can prevent egg **implantation**.</li></ul>
Drugs	<ul><li>Can lead to ovulation problems.</li><li>Long-term drug use can cause permanent damage to the reproductive organs.</li></ul>

Revise it!

- Create flash cards – name a factor on one side (e.g. AGE) and write the gender-specific consequences on the back.
- Choose a card at random and test yourself regularly.

Remember it!

There are five factors that contribute towards pre-conception health: **A**ge **W**eight **S**moking **A**lcohol and **D**rugs (mnemonic: *Amy will surely achieve a distinction*).

Pre-conception health 2 see p. 74

What you need to know

- How pre-conception health affects the chances of conception for men.

Fathers-to-be are affected by the same factors as mothers-to-be, so it's important that both partners consider their health ahead of planned pregnancy.

Five factors affecting **men's** pre-conception health

Age	<ul><li>Men become **fertile** during puberty when they start producing sperm.</li><li>Can father children until old age.</li><li>Sperm quality decreases after the age of 40, which may lead to a higher chance of them fathering a child with a condition, e.g. Down's syndrome.</li></ul>
Weight	<ul><li>Unhealthy diet is linked to low sperm count and low sperm quality.</li><li>Excess weight can interrupt sexual activity, making it difficult to ejaculate inside the **vagina**.</li></ul>
Smoking	<ul><li>Men who smoke tend to have a lower sperm count.</li><li>They also have more abnormal sperm.</li></ul>
Alcohol	<ul><li>Affects the production of **testosterone** leading to **impotence** (not being able to have an erection).</li><li>Can also lead to low sperm count and possibly abnormal sperm.</li></ul>
Drugs	<ul><li>May cause lower sperm count and quality.</li><li>Long-term drug use can cause permanent damage to the reproductive organs.</li></ul>

Practise it!

1. Explain how smoking can affect a woman's pre-conception health. **(2 marks)**
2. State two pre-conception health factors that can result in a man having low sperm count. **(2 marks)**

Remember it!

- Pre-conception health affects fathers-to-be as well as mothers-to-be.
- A man can conceive all his adult life, whilst a woman can only conceive until she reaches the menopause.

Folic acid and immunisations see p. 75

What you need to know

- Why folic acid is recommended for mothers-to-be
- The importance of up-to-date **immunisations**.

Some pre-conception health factors affect only women. It's important to eat a diet rich in folic acid. Because a woman's immune system is weakened during pregnancy, having up-to-date immunisations is very important.

Folic acid (folate)

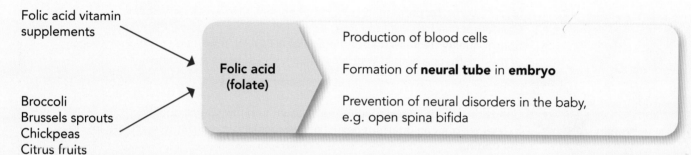

Folic acid vitamin supplements

Broccoli
Brussels sprouts
Chickpeas
Citrus fruits

Folic acid (folate)

Production of blood cells

Formation of **neural tube** in **embryo**

Prevention of neural disorders in the baby, e.g. open spina bifida

Up-to-date immunisations (jabs)

Type of vaccine	Why it is important to have it
Rubella	Women should have this **vaccine** before they get pregnant. It cannot be given during pregnancy.
	There is a high risk of birth defects if a pregnant woman catches rubella, e.g. blindness and/or deafness.
	Catching rubella in pregnancy can also lead to **miscarriage** and **stillbirth**.
Whooping cough	Vaccine can be given during the second **trimester**, passing some of the antibodies to the **foetus**.
	Can help prevent pneumonia and brain damage in babies.
Flu	A pregnant women has a higher risk of developing complications if she catches flu.
	Flu could cause the baby to be born prematurely (before it should be born), have a low birth weight, be stillborn or die.
	The vaccine is safe to have at any stage of pregnancy.
COVID-19	A pregnant woman could pass COVID-19 on to her unborn baby. Immunisation is recommended prior to conception to avoid this. The current guidelines state that a pregnant woman can get vaccinated.

Practise it!

1 Identify *one* possible complication as a result of a woman having a pregnancy diet that is low in folic acid. **(1 mark)**

2 Explain the importance of a woman having up-to-date immunisations for pre-conception health. **(3 marks)**

Remember it!

- Folic acid is necessary for the correct neural tube development of the baby. It prevents spina bifida.
- Rubella and whooping cough are examples of immunisations that should be considered as part of pre-conception health for women.

Barrier methods of contraception see p. 76

- How barrier methods work to prevent pregnancy
- Reasons why people may – or may not – want to use them.

Barrier methods of **contraception** provide a physical obstruction that prevents sperm from reaching the egg. The most common barrier method is a male condom.

Barrier methods of contraception

Method	How it works	Features
Male condom	A man puts it on his erect **penis** before inserting it into the vagina. **Effectiveness: 98%**	+ Protects against STIs + No side effects + Available without prescription − Can slip off or tear − May interrupt sexual pleasure − Single use, so may need a lot of them for regular contraception
Female condom	A woman inserts it in her vagina before intercourse. **Effectiveness: 95%**	
Diaphragm/cap	A woman applies spermicide and places the circular dome inside her vagina, covering the cervix. **Effectiveness: 92–96%**	+ Can be put in place several hours before intercourse + No serious side effects + No need to take any **hormones** − Requires practice to use it correctly − No protection against STIs − Not as easily available; a doctor needs to advise on the correct size

Who might want to use barrier methods?

- Women who cannot use hormonal contraception
- Couples in a new relationship who want to protect themselves from STIs
- Couples who require only occasional contraception
- When hormonal contraception won't work for a period of time, e.g. when a woman is taking the contraceptive pill but needs to take a course of antibiotics that could interfere with its effectiveness.

Practise it!

1 Explain how barrier methods prevent unwanted pregnancy. **(2 marks)**

2 Identify *one* barrier method of contraception that can be used by a woman. **(1 mark)**

Remember it!

- Barrier methods include condoms and diaphragms/caps.
- Not all barrier methods prevent STIs but condoms do.

Non-barrier methods of contraception 1 see p. 77

What you need to know

- How non-barrier methods work to prevent pregnancy
- Reasons why people may – or may not – want to use them.

Non-barrier methods of contraception use hormones or other substances to prevent pregnancy, e.g. by preventing ovulation (the release of an egg).

Contraceptive pills

Method	How it works	Features
POP	Contains synthetic **progesterone** that thickens the mucus, preventing sperm from reaching the egg; it is taken daily. **Effectiveness: over 99%**	+ Doesn't interrupt sexual pleasure + Can be used whilst **breastfeeding** – Only available on prescription – Needs to be taken at the same time every day – May be affected by the use of other medication – Periods may become irregular
Combined pill	Contains synthetic **oestrogen** that stops the egg being released and progesterone that thickens the mucus, holding back the sperm; it is taken daily. **Effectiveness: over 99%**	+ Helps make periods lighter and less painful + Can reduce the risk of some health conditions and diseases, e.g. fibroids, ovarian cysts – Only available on prescription – Not suitable for women over 35 or those who smoke – Needs to be taken at the same time every day – May cause initial side effects, e.g. mood swings and nausea – May increase blood pressure or the likelihood of clots, etc.
Emergency contraceptive pill	A single pill taken after having unprotected sex (up to fifth day); contains high dose of synthetic progesterone that delays or stops ovulation. **Most effective if taken within three days.**	+ Used after sexual intercourse, e.g. if a condom breaks or a woman has forgotten to take a pill – Only available at designated centres/pharmacies – May be affected by the use of other medications – Side effects, e.g. tummy aches and heavy bleeding

Who might want to use pills as a contraceptive method?

- A couple who want reliable protection
- A couple who value uninterrupted sex without visible contraception
- If a couple's usual method of contraception has failed, or they have had unprotected sex, the woman may choose to take the emergency pill.

Revise it!

- Write the name and facts about each contraceptive method on sticky notes.
- Stick them in a visible place to help you revise.

Remember it!

- Hormonal methods use synthetic oestrogen and/or progesterone.
- All hormonal methods require a consultation with a doctor/pharmacist.

Non-barrier methods of contraception 2 see p. 77

What you need to know

- Non-barrier methods as an alternative to taking the pill
- Reasons why people may – or may not – want to use them.

Other ways in which a woman can use hormones to prevent an unwanted pregnancy are: using an **intrauterine** (inside the uterus) coil, or having a contraceptive injection or implant in her arm.

Contraceptive injections, implants and coils

Method	How it works	Features
Contraceptive injection	Contains synthetic progesterone that is released into the bloodstream to prevent ovulation; lasts 8–13 weeks depending on type. **Effectiveness: over 99%**	+ No need to remember to take a daily pill + Safe when breastfeeding – Only available on prescription – May take up to a year for fertility to return to normal – Side effects, e.g. acne, weight gain, mood swings
Contraceptive implant	A small rod inserted under the skin in the arm; it releases synthetic progesterone to prevent ovulation; lasts for three years. **Effectiveness: over 99%**	+ No need to remember to take a daily pill + Safe when breastfeeding + Fertility levels go back to normal once it is removed – Requires a doctor/nurse to put it in and take it out – Initial bruising and tenderness – May cause periods to become irregular
IUD (intrauterine device)	A copper coil is inserted into the uterus; copper alters the chemical balance in the uterus which prevents sperm reaching the egg; lasts 5–10 years. **Effectiveness: over 99%**	+ No need to remember to take a daily pill + No hormonal side effects + In emergency situations, it can be inserted up to five days after unprotected sex – Requires a doctor/nurse to put it in and take it out – May cause heavy periods in the first six months
IUS (intrauterine system)	A small plastic device is inserted into the uterus; it releases synthetic progesterone to prevent ovulation; lasts 3–5 years. **Effectiveness: over 99%**	+ No need to remember to take a daily pill + Safe to use when breastfeeding + Periods may become lighter and less painful – Requires a doctor/nurse to put it in and take it out – Possible hormonal side effects, e.g. mood swings, acne

Who might want to use long-lasting non-barrier methods?

- Established couples who want long-lasting protection
- Women who have given birth and may not want any more children.

Practise it!

1 Explain how a contraceptive implant prevents unwanted pregnancy. **(2 marks)**
2 Outline *two* disadvantages of using an IUS as a method of contraception. **(2 marks)**

Remember it!

- Out of the two intrauterine options, only the IUS releases hormones.
- None of these non-barrier methods of contraception protect against STIs.

Natural family planning see p. 79

- Three methods used as part of NFP.

NFP is used when a woman is aware of her **menstrual cycle** and plans to have sex on the days in which she is less fertile (and therefore less likely to get pregnant) to avoid unwanted pregnancy.

Three methods

Temperature method

The woman takes her temperature every morning and keeps a record of it. Ovulation happens when there is a slight increase in body temperature; after having a raised temperature for three days, the following days in the cycle are considered to be 'safe', so a couple could have unprotected sex.

Cervical mucus method

The woman observes the mucus secretion on her underwear. Around ovulation, it becomes clear and slippery, which is when a woman is most fertile. Once it becomes thicker and creamier, fertility levels fall, and a couple could have unprotected sex.

Calendar method

The woman tracks her period. Ovulation happens around two weeks before a woman's period (days 14–16 of a typical cycle). As sperm live for up to seven days, it is best to avoid sex five to seven days before the day of ovulation, and two days after.

Evaluation and effectiveness

All three methods combined, if used correctly, are **up to 99% effective**, meaning only one woman out of 100 would accidentally get pregnant. Below are some strengths and weaknesses of NFP:

+ Accepted by all religions/cultures
+ No side effects
+ No need for regular pill prescriptions

– Takes time to learn and practise
– A couple can only have sex on certain days
– Doesn't protect against STIs

Practise it!

1 Outline *one* method used as part of natural family planning. **(2 marks)**

2 Discuss *two* disadvantages of natural family planning. **(4 marks)**

Remember it!

NFP is the only contraceptive method accepted by all religions.

Female reproductive system 1 see p. 80

What you need to know

- Identify different elements of the system: **ovaries**, **fallopian tubes**, uterus/womb, cervix, vagina
- Know their role in the process of conception.

'Reproductive system' describes the organs and tissues involved in the process of **reproduction**. The male reproductive system is revised separately.

Five parts of the female reproductive system

Ovary (plural: ovaries)
- Eggs mature here – usually one egg is released each month (ovulation)
- Produces the hormones oestrogen and progesterone

Fallopian tube
- Carries sperm to the egg
- Conception happens here, i.e. the egg meets the sperm
- Transports the egg to the uterus

Cervix
- Produces mucus that protects the uterus and helps sperm move
- Opens for menstrual periods
- Widens during **labour**

Uterus (womb)
- Lining thickens each month in preparation to receive a fertilised egg
- Lining sheds every month (as a woman's menstrual period)
- A fertilised egg implants here
- Contains, protects and nourishes the foetus and **placenta**
- Expands during pregnancy

Vagina
- Penis enters the vagina during intercourse
- Holds sperm before it passes into the uterus
- A birth channel for the baby

Usually, a single egg is released every month from alternating ovaries. This process is called ovulation.

Revise it!

- To help you learn the correct spelling, write the names of the reproductive parts with missing letters on to a set of mini cards or slips of paper.
- Test yourself by filling in the missing letters.

Remember it!

- Conception (when a sperm fertilises an egg) happens in the fallopian tube.
- Oestrogen and progesterone are the female sex hormones. They are released by the ovaries.

Female reproductive system 2 see p. 81

What you need to know

- What happens during the menstrual cycle
- Understand a diagram of the menstrual cycle and identify the fertile and less fertile days.

The menstrual cycle starts on the first day of a woman's menstrual period and lasts, on average, for 28 days.

Phases of a typical 28-day menstrual cycle

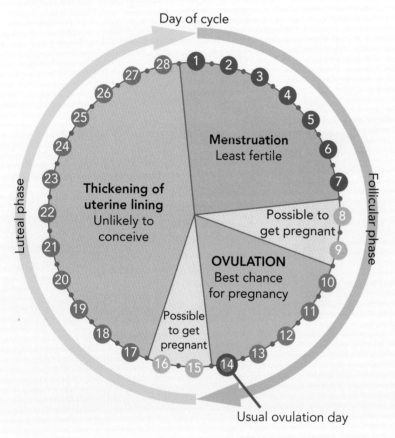

Usual ovulation day

Key points to learn

- Menstrual cycles differ from woman to woman but a typical menstrual cycle is 28 days.
- The medical word for a period is '**menstruation**'. This takes place in the first five days of the menstrual cycle.
- Ovulation (the release of an egg and a surge in oestrogen) happens at around day 14. This is when a woman is at her most fertile and most likely to become pregnant.
- The egg only lives for few hours but sperm can live for several days. This is why there are a few days before and after ovulation when a woman is still very likely to get pregnant.
- Most of the less fertile days (when a woman is less likely to get pregnant) fall in the second half of the cycle.
- If **fertilisation** doesn't take place, progesterone levels drop and the body prepares to menstruate.

Practise it!

1   Outline *two* functions of the ovaries.
                                    (2 marks)

2   Explain which days are the most fertile in a typical 28-day menstrual cycle.   **(3 marks)**

Remember it!

- Ovulation usually happens on day 14 of a typical 28-day menstrual cycle.
- Fertile days are usually counted as being seven days before ovulation and two days afterwards.

Revision Guide

Male reproductive system see p. 82

What you need to know

- Identify the different parts of the system: penis, **testes/testicles**, **sperm duct/epididymis**, **vas deferens**, **seminal vesicles** and **urethra**, and know their role in the process of conception.

Adult men stay fertile all their lives. Unlike women, they are not dependent on monthly cycles and can produce active sperm at any time of the day.

Six parts of the male reproductive system

Seminal vesicle
- One of a pair of glands that release a nutritious fluid that mixes with sperm to produce semen

Vas deferens
- Takes sperm to the urethra, before ejaculation

Urethra
- A tube which carries urine and semen (not at the same time!) out of the penis

Sperm duct/epididymis
- Sperm matures here
- Carries sperm from the testes to the vas deferens

Penis
- Used to ejaculate sperm during sexual intercourse and for urination

Testes (testicle)
- Enclosed in a skin sac called a scrotum
- Produce and store sperm
- Produce the male sex hormone testosterone

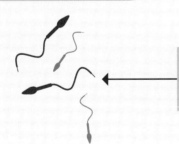

In one ejaculation, a man releases millions of sperm suspended in a liquid called semen

Practise it!

1 Outline *two* functions of the testes.
(2 marks)

2 Draw a diagram showing the journey of sperm from the testes to the penis. Label the different organs involved in the process. (5 marks)

Remember it!

- Sperm are male reproductive cells, whilst semen is the fluid that carries the sperm out of the man's body.
- Testosterone is the male sex hormone. It is released by the testes.

How reproduction takes place 1 see p. 83

What you need to know

- Understand the process of conception (fertilisation), i.e. when and where it takes place.

Conception – the joining of an egg and a sperm – happens in the fallopian tube.

Sexual intercourse

A couple should time their sexual activity around ovulation if they wish to conceive. This ensures that the woman is at her most fertile.

Sperm travels from the testes, through the vas deferens, through the urethra and out into the vagina

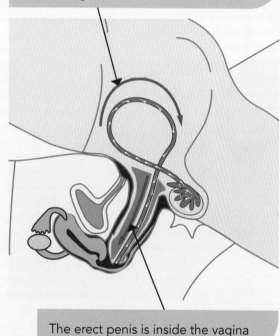

The erect penis is inside the vagina

Conception (fertilisation)

2   After 30–45 minutes, some of the sperm reaches the fallopian tube

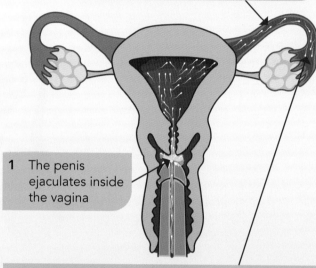

1   The penis ejaculates inside the vagina

3   If sexual intercourse takes place around the time of ovulation, the sperm may fertilise the egg. Conception usually takes place inside the fallopian tube

Sex of the baby

The sex of a baby is determined during conception. If a Y sperm fertilises the egg, it will be a boy (XY). If an X sperm fertilises the egg, the baby will be a girl (XX).

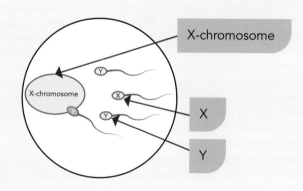

X-chromosome

X-chromosome

X

Y

Revise it!

Using the diagrams, write down what happens during reproduction. The first step has been given to help you.

1   *The erect penis enters the vagina.*

Remember it!

- The egg and sperm meet in the fallopian tube and this is where fertilisation takes place.
- Combination of chromosomes XX will result in a girl being born, XY in a boy.

How reproduction takes place 2 see p. 83

What you need to know

- How and when implantation happens.

Implantation is when a fertilised egg burrows into the lining of the uterus.
It happens approximately a week after conception.

Implantation

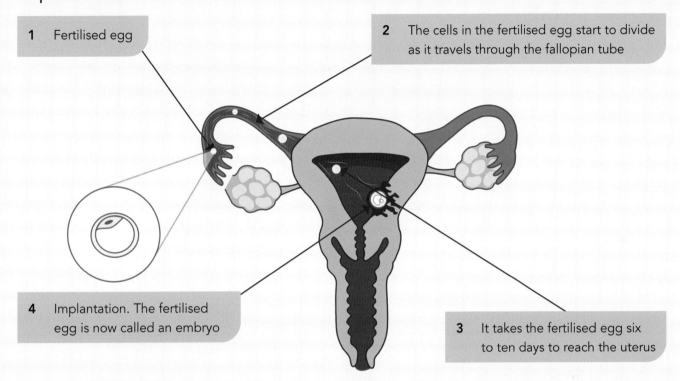

1   Fertilised egg

2   The cells in the fertilised egg start to divide as it travels through the fallopian tube

4   Implantation. The fertilised egg is now called an embryo

3   It takes the fertilised egg six to ten days to reach the uterus

Key points to learn

- Fertilisation happens in the fallopian tube.
- The male sperm determines the sex of the baby.
- Thanks to tiny hair-like structures inside the fallopian tube, the fertilised egg travels towards the uterus. As it travels, it goes through a process of cell division.

- After six to ten days, the fertilised egg reaches the uterus and burrows into the lining of the uterus.
- Some women experience minor pain and bleeding (spotting) when implantation happens.
- The implanted fertilised egg is now called an embryo.

Practise it!

1   What is meant by 'implantation'? **(1 mark)**
2   Outline what happens to an egg after it is fertilised.   **(2 marks)**

Remember it!

- A fertilised egg implants itself into the lining of the uterus.
- After implantation, the new life is called an embryo.

Development of the embryo and foetus see p. 84

What you need to know

- The difference between an embryo and foetus
- The structures associated with pregnancy: **amniotic fluid**, **umbilical cord** and placenta.

The developing baby is known as an embryo from implantation to around the eighth week of pregnancy; after this point, it is called a foetus.

Pregnant uterus

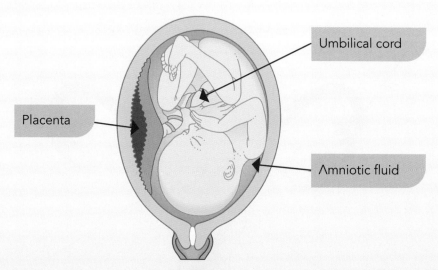

Structure	Description	Functions
Amniotic fluid	Transparent liquid inside a sac that surrounds the embryo/foetus	• Protects the embryo/foetus (acts as a cushion and contains antibodies) • Maintains a constant temperature inside the womb • Helps muscle development as the foetus/embryo can move freely in the uterus • Lubricates the embryo/foetus to prevent webbed fingers and toes
Umbilical cord	A tube that connects the embryo/foetus to the pregnant woman's placenta	• Transfers oxygen and nutrients from the placenta to the baby • Transfers waste products (e.g. carbon dioxide, urea) away from the baby
Placenta	A temporary organ that supports the foetus/embryo; it is attached to the wall of the uterus, usually at the top or side	• Produces important hormones that support the pregnancy • Supplies nutrients and oxygen for the baby, which are transferred by the umbilical cord • Filters waste products from the embryo/foetus • Separates the pregnant woman's and the baby's blood

Practise it!

1 Explain the difference between an embryo and a foetus. **(2 marks)**
2 Outline *two* functions of the placenta. **(2 marks)**

Remember it!

- The umbilical cord connects the baby to the placenta, allowing the exchange of nutrients and oxygen.
- It also takes away the waste products.

Multiple pregnancies see p. 85

What you need to know

- How multiple pregnancies occur
- The difference between **identical twins** and **non-identical twins**.

Multiple pregnancies can occur naturally or as a result of fertility treatment such as IVF. Two babies are called twins, three babies are called triplets, and four babies are called quadruplets.

Identical twins

Identical twins come from a single egg fertilised with a single sperm. The fertilised egg splits during or shortly after fertilisation.

They share the same genes, so they will be the same sex and have the same characteristics (like eye or hair colour). They share a placenta.

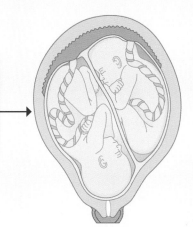

Non-identical twins

Non-identical twins come from two or more eggs, each fertilised by a different sperm. Sometimes a woman's ovaries release two or more eggs during ovulation.

These twins have different sets of genes, meaning that they may be different sexes (a boy and a girl) and will look different. They will each have their own placenta in the uterus.

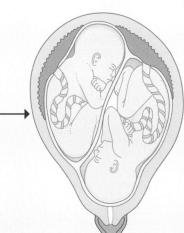

Risks involved in multiple pregnancies

- Most multiple pregnancies are delivered prematurely, often needing a C-section.
- Less space to grow and problems with sharing nutrients can lead to low birth weight.
- Increased risk of the babies being born with abnormalities, like open spina bifida.
- Increased risk of miscarriage.
- Greater strain on the pregnant woman's body.

Practise it!

1. Explain how identical twins are formed. **(2 marks)**
2. State *one* feature of a non-identical twin pregnancy. **(1 mark)**

Remember it!

Identical twins share one placenta, whilst non-identical twins each have their own placenta.

Signs and symptoms of pregnancy see p. 86

What you need to know

- Five common **signs** and **symptoms** of pregnancy: breast changes, missed period, nausea, passing urine more frequently and tiredness.

A woman's body goes through a lot of changes in the first weeks of pregnancy, mainly due to the increased production of two hormones: progesterone and hCG (human chorionic gonadotropin).

Five signs and symptoms of pregnancy

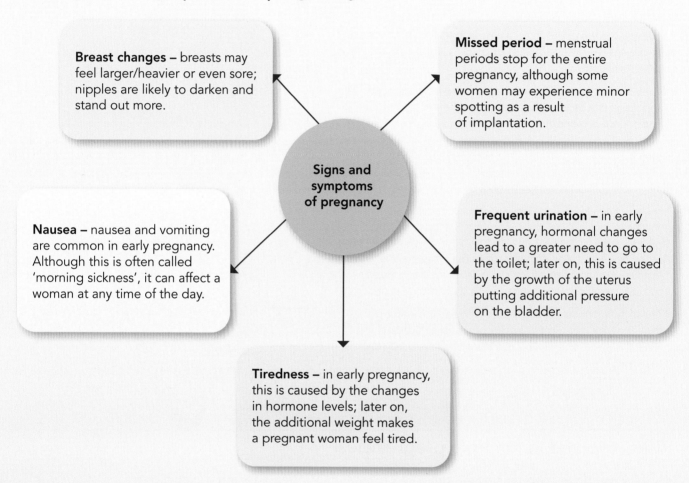

Breast changes – breasts may feel larger/heavier or even sore; nipples are likely to darken and stand out more.

Missed period – menstrual periods stop for the entire pregnancy, although some women may experience minor spotting as a result of implantation.

Signs and symptoms of pregnancy

Nausea – nausea and vomiting are common in early pregnancy. Although this is often called 'morning sickness', it can affect a woman at any time of the day.

Frequent urination – in early pregnancy, hormonal changes lead to a greater need to go to the toilet; later on, this is caused by the growth of the uterus putting additional pressure on the bladder.

Tiredness – in early pregnancy, this is caused by the changes in hormone levels; later on, the additional weight makes a pregnant woman feel tired.

Practise it!

1 Describe how a woman's breasts change in the early weeks of pregnancy. **(2 marks)**

2 Outline *two* other common symptoms of pregnancy. **(2 marks)**

Remember it!

There are five main signs/symptoms of pregnancy: **b**reast changes, **m**issed period, **n**ausea, **f**requent urination, **t**iredness (mnemonic: *baby's mother needs further testing* – and indeed, she should do a pregnancy test!).

Professionals involved in antenatal care see p. 87

- Definition of the term 'antenatal'
- Roles of different health professionals involved in pregnancy.

Antenatal means 'before birth', so **antenatal care** is the healthcare a woman receives when she is pregnant. An **antenatal clinic** is where pregnancy appointments take place.

Health professionals involved in pregnancy care

General practitioner (GP)
The family doctor, who knows the pregnant woman's medical history and can refer her to specialist care if needed

Midwife
A specialist nurse who is trained to assist women during pregnancy, deliver a baby and offer short-term care after the birth

Obstetrician
A doctor who specialises in pregnancy and labour. They are called to attend more complex cases

How they support pregnant women

- Arranges tests to confirm the pregnancy
- Consults her about pre-existing health conditions and family history
- Treats associated problems, e.g. flu, anaemia
- Refers her to a specialist if needed
- Advises on contraception after giving birth

- Arranges all clinical examinations, including **screening tests**, as required
- Regularly monitors the health of the pregnant woman and her baby
- Delivers parenting classes
- Leads the labour process, including the delivery of the baby
- Offers women care after they give birth, but only for a short time

- Assists/advises in difficult pregnancies, e.g. babies with spina bifida
- Performs C-sections and other related surgeries if required
- Decides on medication that a midwife may not be qualified to prescribe

Practise it!

1. Outline *two* functions of a GP in antenatal care. **(2 marks)**
2. Explain how an obstetrician supports a pregnant woman. **(3 marks)**

Remember it!

Even though midwives deliver most babies, they are not doctors, and rely on the advice of an obstetrician if there are complications with a pregnancy.

Antenatal clinic appointments 1 see p. 88

What you need to know

- Timing of the first antenatal appointment.

The first antenatal appointment takes place eight to ten weeks into a pregnancy. After this, a pregnant woman consults her midwife regularly for routine checks.

What happens at the first appointment with the midwife

The midwife interviews the pregnant woman and asks her about:

- any previous pregnancies or miscarriages
- the date of her last period
- any genetic diseases running in the family
- her general physical health, including diet, exercise, medication, drugs, drinking or smoking
- her mental health
- her work life and her home life.

EDD (estimated due date) is calculated. This is when the baby is expected to be born. It is roughly estimated by adding 280 days to the first day of the pregnant woman's last period.

A blood sample is taken to check:

- what the pregnant woman's blood group is in case she needs a blood transfusion during labour
- her rhesus factor in case there are harmful antibodies that conflict with baby's blood group
- her iron levels in case she has anaemia (iron deficiency).

Due to a high chance of early miscarriage, the first appointment would not be scheduled earlier than the eighth week of pregnancy.

Revise it!

Create a list of questions a midwife would ask a pregnant woman on her first visit, e.g. *When did your last period start?*

Remember it!

The first midwife appointment should happen between week 8 and week 10 of pregnancy.

Antenatal clinic appointments 2 see p. 88

- Routine checks and reasons why they are performed.

Routine checks are done regularly on most antenatal clinic visits. They are important as they help to monitor the pregnant woman's health.

Routine tests/checks

What is checked	Why it is checked
Baby's heartbeat	To check that the baby is alive and not distressed. A regular healthy heartbeat in an unborn baby should be within the range of 110–160 beats per minute.
Blood pressure	The pregnant woman's blood pressure is checked. High blood pressure could be a sign that a woman has developed **pre-eclampsia** and may need medication.
Blood tests (samples)	During the first visit, a blood sample will identify the pregnant woman's blood group and rhesus factor. Blood tests are used to check the pregnant woman's levels of haemoglobin and iron in order to prevent anaemia (iron deficiency). They also check for infectious diseases and more serious pregnancy complications, like Down's syndrome.
Uterus examination	This is done by measuring from the top of the woman's abdomen to the pubic bone. It helps the midwife see if the baby is growing as expected according to the number of weeks of pregnancy. The midwife can also touch the belly to check the baby's movements and position – this is particularly important closer to labour to confirm that the baby is not *breeched* (breech position means the baby is head up in opposite to head down).
Urine tests	A sample is checked for protein and glucose traces. It can help to detect pre-eclampsia, **gestational diabetes** and urinary tract infections.
Weight checks	A pregnant woman is monitored to check that she is gaining weight as expected and that the baby is growing normally. If too much weight is gained, this can indicate pre-eclampsia, gestational diabetes or unhealthy habits that need changing. Weight loss can be a sign that the baby is not growing (or has died) or that the pregnant woman is suffering from illness.

Practise it!

1. Name *two* routine checks performed during antenatal visits. **(2 marks)**
2. Explain the importance of weight checks in antenatal appointments. **(2 marks)**

Remember it!

Some of the complications that can be spotted in routine antenatal tests include: pre-eclampsia, anaemia and pregnancy diabetes.

Screening tests see p. 89

- When screening tests take place
- The reasons for having screening tests and the conditions they can identify.

Screening tests are used to check the development of the foetus and to identify the risk of specific health conditions. They are offered to all pregnant women.

Screening tests

Blood tests

Non-Invasive Prenatal Testing (NIPT)

- Has to be paid for privately.
- Can be done as early as week 10 until the end of the pregnancy.
- Looks for genetic mutations and chromosomal abnormalities, e.g. Down's syndrome.

Triple test

- Offered by the NHS between weeks 10 and 14 of pregnancy.
- In some cases, can be done up to week 20.
- Mainly used to check for three chromosomal disorders, i.e. Down's syndrome, Edwards' syndrome, Patau's syndrome.

Ultrasound scans

Dating scan

- The first scan takes place between weeks 10 and 14.
- The sonographer (the person who does the scan) checks the size and growth of the baby and confirms the EDD.
- Shows whether it is a single or multiple (e.g. twins) pregnancy.
- The second scan can usually confirm the sex of the baby.

Nuchal fold translucency (NFT) scan

- Usually takes place between weeks 11 and 14.
- Usually offered alongside the first dating scan.
- The sonographer measures the thickness of the nuchal (neck) fold to check the likelihood of the baby having Down's syndrome (thicker fold = higher chances).

Anomaly scan

- Takes place between weeks 18 and 21.
- As well as checking the growth and development of the baby, the sonographer looks for 11 rare conditions, e.g. cleft lip/palate, anencephaly, open spina bifida or serious cardiac (heart) problems.

Revise it!

Create flash cards with the name of the test on one side and details on the other. Test yourself regularly.

Remember it!

NIPT and the triple test are blood tests, whilst the dating scan, NFT and anomaly scan are tested with an ultrasound device.

Diagnostic tests see p. 89

see p. 89

- When **diagnostic tests** take place
- The reasons for having diagnostic tests and the conditions they can identify.

These are special tests which can confirm whether or not an unborn baby has a condition/problem shown in a screening test. Not all pregnant women have diagnostic tests.

Amniocentesis

- Usually takes place between weeks 15 and 20 of the pregnancy.
- A sample of amniotic fluid is taken from around the baby.
- It is invasive (goes into the body), which means it can potentially cause a miscarriage.
- Confirms if the baby has a genetic or chromosomal abnormality, e.g. Down's syndrome.

Chorionic villus sampling (CVS)

- Can be done between weeks 11 and 14.
- May be recommended for women with a higher health risk, e.g. older mothers.
- A sample is taken from the placenta.
- It confirms if the baby has a genetic or chromosomal abnormality, e.g. cystic fibrosis.

Examples of conditions that can be identified in screening/diagnostic tests

- **Cleft lip/palate** – this happens when parts of the upper lip do not form properly.
- **Down's syndrome** – caused by having by an extra chromosome; it causes learning difficulties which can be mild to severe.
- **Cystic fibrosis** – a genetic disorder that affects the lungs and digestive system. It worsens with age.
- **Open spina bifida** – a serious neural tube birth defect caused when the spine and spinal cord do not form correctly in early pregnancy.

Practise it!

1   Outline what is checked during a dating scan. **(2 marks)**
2   Name *one* diagnostic test that can be offered to a woman in pregnancy. **(1 mark)**

Remember it!

Some of the conditions that can be confirmed by a diagnostic test include: Down's syndrome, cystic fibrosis, open spina bifida.

Antenatal (parenting) classes 1 see p. 91

What you need to know

- Main topics covered during antenatal classes
- Benefits of the father/partner attending parenting classes.

Antenatal classes are often led by community midwives either on behalf of the NHS or privately. Pregnant women and their partners usually attend classes in the last trimester (three months) of their pregnancy.

Purpose of antenatal classes

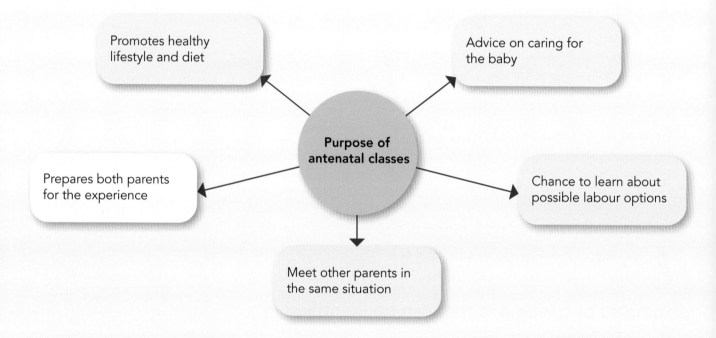

Promotes healthy lifestyle and diet

Advice on caring for the baby

Purpose of antenatal classes

Prepares both parents for the experience

Chance to learn about possible labour options

Meet other parents in the same situation

It is not only mums-to-be who benefit from antenatal classes. Here is a list of benefits for fathers/partners:

- Can offer emotional support to the mother by being involved.
- Learn how to help care for the baby once they're born.
- Learn how to support their partner in labour, e.g. massaging techniques, counting **contractions**.
- Can have their questions answered and discuss their concerns.
- Can socialise with other parents and create friendship groups.

Revise it!

Create two spidergrams – one showing the benefits for a pregnant woman and the other showing the benefits for a father/partner of attending antenatal classes. Remember that a partner may not be the father of a child. Make a list of alternative partners who may be involved.

Remember it!

- Antenatal classes are offered in the third trimester of pregnancy.
- They educate pregnant women and their partners about pregnancy, labour and how to care for a baby.

Revision Guide

Antenatal (parenting) classes 2 see p. 91

- Food to avoid during pregnancy
- Antenatal classes promote a healthy lifestyle in pregnancy.

Pregnant women should eat a healthy **balanced diet**. There are some foods that pregnant women should avoid as they can pose a danger to the pregnancy.

Food to avoid during pregnancy

Food to avoid	Why it should be avoided
Unpasteurised milk products, e.g. brie	Milk that hasn't been heat processed can contain listeria, which is a type of **bacteria**. **Listeriosis** (an illness caused by listeria) can lead to miscarriage or stillbirth.
Undercooked, raw or cured meat Unwashed fruit and vegetables	Can carry a common parasite that causes an infection called **toxoplasmosis**; it is not harmful to healthy adults, but in pregnancy it can affect the baby's brain development and lead to miscarriage or stillbirth.
Raw or partially cooked eggs, unless they are British Lion stamped	**Salmonella** poisoning from eggs can lead to low levels of amniotic fluid, birth defects and even miscarriage or stillbirth.
Caffeine	High levels of caffeine have been linked to low birth weight, miscarriage and stillbirth.
Liver and liver products, e.g. pâté	Liver contains high levels of vitamin A, which can affect a developing foetus and lead to birth defects in the nervous system.
Raw shellfish, too much tuna, too much oily fish	Raw shellfish and seafood can contain bacteria that are harmful to a developing baby. Tuna contains higher levels of **mercury** than other types of fish and should be eaten in moderation. Pregnant women should have no more than two portions of oily fish a week.
Alcohol	Alcohol should be avoided altogether as it can lead to **foetal alcohol syndrome** (FAS), which affects the internal organs of a baby as well as their intellectual development.

Having a healthy lifestyle during pregnancy

- Do 'safe' exercises, e.g. **pelvic floor exercises** that strengthen the lower muscles around a person's bladder, bottom, and a woman's vagina or a man's penis.
- Avoid risky sports that could lead to a fall, e.g. horse riding, skiing.
- Avoid stress and get the right amount of sleep.
- Avoid pollution, quit smoking and avoid being a passive smoker.

Revise it!

Create a poster showing all the food items that should be avoided during pregnancy and the reasons why. Share it with your subject teacher.

Remember it!

Listeria could be caught from unpasteurised dairy products; toxoplasmosis could be caught from undercooked meat; and salmonella could be caught from raw eggs that don't carry the British Lion stamp.

Antenatal (parenting) classes 3 see p. 91

- Advice given on caring for a baby at an antenatal class
- Advice on feeding, including reasons for breastfeeding.

As well as preparing pregnant women and their partners for pregnancy and birth, antenatal classes give them advice on how to look after a baby.

Caring for a baby

At antenatal classes, expectant parents learn how to:

- change a nappy and the differences between **disposable nappies** and **reusable nappies**
- wash a baby, including **topping and tailing** (cleaning the baby using cotton wool and a bowl of warm water rather than putting them in a bath)
- breastfeed and **bottle-feed**, what equipment is needed, and the problems that may occur.

Breastfeeding a newborn

Mothers are encouraged to breastfeed a baby in the first two weeks of their life. This is because:

- the mother's milk has colostrum – a nutritious substance full of antibodies that helps to build up the baby's immune system
- when the baby sucks the mother's breast, hormones are released that help the uterus shrink to its pre-pregnancy size
- it decreases mother's risk for some cancers, **obesity** and osteoporosis (weak bones)
- it reduces the risk of the baby having an upset stomach and **SIDS**.
- Continued breastfeeding reduces the risk of future health problems for the child.
- it is a bonding time for the mother and the baby, helping to form parental attachment.

Possible problems with breastfeeding include:

- not enough or too much milk being produced
- blocked milk ducts
- baby doesn't latch (attach) to the breast properly
- sore or cracked nipples
- breast infections, e.g. mastitis (inflammation of the breast), an abscess or thrush.

Practise it!

1 Name a food item high in vitamin A that should be avoided in pregnancy. **(1 mark)**

2 Outline *two* benefits of choosing breastfeeding as the first feeding method. **(2 marks)**

Remember it!

Topping and tailing is an alternative to a bath, where a baby would be cleaned with warm water and cotton wools.

Choices available for delivery: hospital birth see p. 93

What you need to know

- Reasons for choosing a hospital birth
- Advantages and disadvantages of a hospital birth.

Usually, a pregnant woman includes information about where she wants to give birth and what type of pain relief she may wish to use in her **birth plan**.

A hospital birth is usually recommended for first-time mothers. Hospital births are also encouraged if complications have been identified (e.g. multiple pregnancy, breech position) or if the pregnant woman has a health condition that needs to be monitored (e.g. high blood pressure, epilepsy). Also, some couples may not have ideal home conditions for a home birth and may prefer labour to take place in a hospital where everything will be provided.

Look at the list of advantages and disadvantages of a hospital birth:

+

- Sterile (clean) environment
- Wide range of pain relief available (e.g. **epidural**)
- Access to trained medical staff, e.g. paediatrician, obstetrician
- Access to specialist equipment if something goes wrong (e.g. incubator for the baby)
- Chance to meet other mothers and share the experience
- No need to worry about cooking and cleaning
- Time to recover after birth

−

- Visitors may be restricted
- Some mothers find the hospital environment noisy and uncomfortable
- The lead midwife may not be the same person the mother is used to
- Not much privacy
- Hospital may be far away from the pregnant woman's home
- Chance of catching an infection, e.g. COVID-19, hepatitis
- Few personal belongings

Revise it!

Cut a piece of paper into narrow strips. Write one advantage or disadvantage on each strip for home births and hospital births. Fold up the strips of paper. Pick a strip. Test yourself – can you say whether it refers to a home birth or a hospital birth?

Remember it!

One benefit of a hospital birth is having access to specialist equipment, such as incubators.

Choices available for delivery: home birth see p. 93

What you need to know

- Reasons for choosing a home birth
- Advantages and disadvantages of home birth.

A pregnant woman may consider a home birth if she feels it is right for her, as long as the pregnancy is straightforward and a home birth is considered to be safe. It may be less stressful than a hospital birth.

A home birth may be considered by pregnant women who do not expect any complications, especially those who have given birth before. It's essential that the home meets certain requirements, e.g. access to clean, hot water, and a large, ventilated room. The pregnant woman and her partner also need to provide waterproof sheets and extra towels. It is possible to rent a birthing pool and have it set up in the house.

Look at the advantages and disadvantages of a home birth:

+	−
• A familiar place, with all personal items available • No need to travel to the hospital • Unrestricted number of visitors, including the baby's older siblings • The woman will not be separated from her partner after the birth • A familiar midwife will assist the delivery • More privacy as there are no strangers or other babies crying	• Some pain relief (e.g. epidural) is not available at home • No specialist equipment or doctors if there are complications during labour • Cooking and cleaning needs to be done • Has to be prepared in advance, e.g. buy extra towels • The home environment may not be as clean/sterile as the hospital environment • The mother is less likely to rest after labour

Practise it!

1 Outline *two* advantages of a hospital birth. **(2 marks)**

2 Explain *one* reason why it may be recommended for someone to have a hospital birth rather than home birth. **(2 marks)**

Remember it!

Certain types of pain relief, like an epidural, cannot be given at home.

The role of the birth partner see p. 94

- The physical and emotional support that can be given by the birth partner
- The benefits of having a birth partner.

A pregnant woman can have a birth partner with her during labour. Typically, it is the father of the baby, but not always. She may have a friend or a relative with her.

Physical support offered by the birth partner

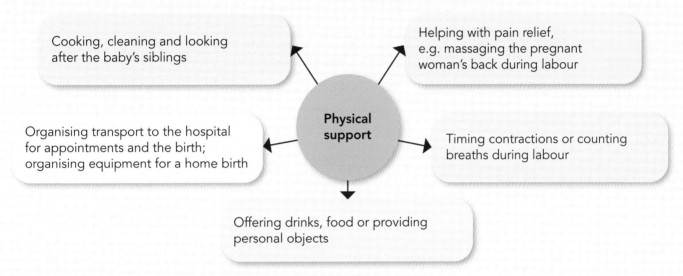

Cooking, cleaning and looking after the baby's siblings

Helping with pain relief, e.g. massaging the pregnant woman's back during labour

Physical support

Organising transport to the hospital for appointments and the birth; organising equipment for a home birth

Timing contractions or counting breaths during labour

Offering drinks, food or providing personal objects

Emotional support offered by the birth partner

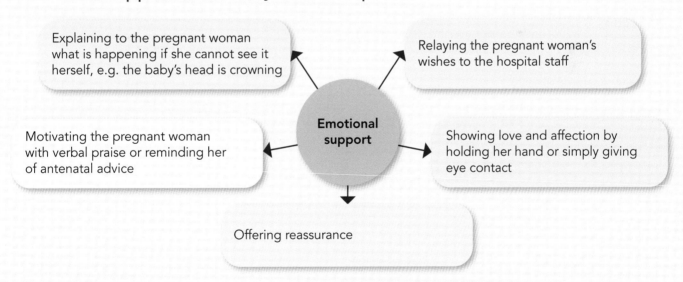

Explaining to the pregnant woman what is happening if she cannot see it herself, e.g. the baby's head is crowning

Relaying the pregnant woman's wishes to the hospital staff

Emotional support

Motivating the pregnant woman with verbal praise or reminding her of antenatal advice

Showing love and affection by holding her hand or simply giving eye contact

Offering reassurance

Practise it!

1 Give *two* examples of possible birth partners. **(2 marks)**
2 Outline *one* benefit of having a birth partner during labour. **(1 mark)**

Remember it!

Distinguish between physical support, e.g. massaging the pregnant woman's back or counting contractions, and emotional support, e.g. giving praise or reassuring her.

Pain relief in labour 1 see p. 95

What you need to know

- Advantages and disadvantages of an epidural and Entonox (pain releif).

Epidurals and Entonox are types of **anaesthetic**.

Epidural

What is it?	Who can give it?	Can it be used in a home birth?
A numbing injection. It goes into the spine.	A specialist doctor	No

Strengths	Weaknesses
Almost always gives total pain relief	Can cause a drop in the woman's blood pressure
Can be used for C-sections	The woman may struggle to move her legs or pass urine
Doesn't affect the baby	It's difficult for the woman to feel contractions, which can extend labour
	Cannot be used during a water birth

Entonox (gas and air)

What is it?	Who can give it?	Can it be used in a home birth?
A mixture of gas and air inhaled through a mask or mouthpiece	The woman giving birth controls when she gets it	Yes

Strengths	Weaknesses
Helps regulate the woman's breathing	Can make the woman feel lightheaded/drowsy and sick
Doesn't affect the baby	Can cause dry lips and thirst
Can be used during a water birth	Not very effective; only some pain will be relieved; wears off quickly
Easy and quick to use	
Controlled by the woman giving birth	

Revise it!

There are four methods of pain relief in total. Create a table to compare the strengths and weaknesses of epidurals and Entonox. Later, add pethidine and TENS to your table.

Remember it!

- Epidural can only be given by a specialist doctor.
- Entonox is the medical name for gas and air.

Pain relief in labour 2 see p. 95

- Advantages and disadvantages of pethidine and TENS.

Pethidine

What is it?	Who can give it?	Can it be used in a home birth?
An anaesthetic that is injected into the thigh	A midwife or doctor	Yes

Strengths	Weaknesses
Effective in relieving most of the pain	Can only be used in the first stage of labour as it can affect the baby, causing difficulties in breathing and feeding if given too close to delivery
Helps the woman to relax	Can cause the woman to feel sick/dizzy
	Cannot be used during a water birth

TENS (transcutaneous electrical nerve stimulation)

What is it?	Who can give it?	Can it be used in a home birth?
Electric pads are attached to the woman's back that which send impulses that block the transmission of pain to the brain	The woman giving birth controls when she gets it	Yes

Strengths	Weaknesses
No side effects for the woman or the baby	Shouldn't be used if the woman has epilepsy or heart problems
Controlled by the woman	Cannot be used during a water birth
The woman is fully conscious and can move around	Limited pain relief

Practise it!

1 Outline *two* strengths of Entonox as a method of pain relief during labour. **(2 marks)**
2 Explain *one* reason why a woman may decide not to use pethidine. **(2 marks)**

Remember it!

TENS is the safest option for most women. Unfortunately, it doesn't relieve all the pain.

Signs that labour has started see p. 97

What you need to know

- Three signs that labour has started: a show, waters breaking and contractions.

Typically, labour happens in week 40 of a pregnancy. The start is often called the onset of labour. It is recognised by three main signs: a **show**, **waters breaking** and contractions.

Three signs that labour has started

Contractions
Contractions mean that the uterus is preparing to push. The muscles tighten for a minute or so and then relax. Contractions may differ in intensity and frequency, and at the beginning may be irregular. As the labour progresses, they become more intense and regular. Initially, they may resemble period pain or back pain. It's good if the woman or her birth partner can keep track of the frequency of contractions.

Three signs labour has started

A show
Having a show means that the plug of mucus in the cervix has been released. A woman would see a sticky, pink (sometimes blood-stained) substance coming out of her vagina. It is a sign that the cervix has started to open in preparation for labour.

Waters breaking
Waters breaking means that the amniotic fluid has been released from the amniotic sac. In some cases, there may be a lot of fluid, whilst some women experience only a little. It is a sign that the woman needs to go to hospital unless she has planned a home birth.

Revise it!

To help you memorise the three elements of the onset of labour, create a rhyme for each of them. Here's one to start you off: *Without a show, there is no go. If the cervix doesn't open, then the labour cannot happen.*

Remember it!

When we say 'waters breaking', we mean the amniotic fluid being released from the amniotic sac.

Stages of labour see p. 97

What you need to know

- The three stages of labour and what happens at each stage.

Labour has three stages. Stage 2 is when the baby is born.

Three stages of labour

Stage 1 Neck of the uterus opens	• Cervix softens and slowly dilates (opens) • Contractions are five to ten minutes apart • Finishes when the cervix is fully dilated (around 10 cm) 
Stage 2 Birth	• Contractions are regular – usually two to three minutes apart and more intense • Woman pushes to move baby down the birth canal • Baby's head is visible in the birth canal (crowning) • Baby is born – usally head first 
Stage 3 Delivery of placenta	• Contractions continue • Umbilical cord is cut • The mother may be given an injection of synthetic oxytocin to help her deliver the placenta more quickly and to prevent heavy bleeding • Placenta detaches from the uterus and exits through the vagina. 

Practise it!

1 Outline *one* sign that labour has started. **(2 marks)**
2 Briefly explain what happens in stage 3 of labour. **(2 marks)**

Remember it!

- Stage 1: neck of the uterus opens, cervix dilates.
- Stage 2: baby is born.
- Stage 3: placenta is delivered.

Assisted birth 1 see p. 98

What you need to know

- How each **instrumental delivery** method is carried out
- Why an **assisted birth** may be necessary.

Sometimes medical intervention is necessary. Most methods of assisted birth can only be carried out in a hospital by an obstetrician, and consent will be needed from the woman.

Instrumental delivery

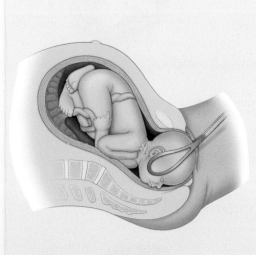

Forceps

What: A metal instrument with two handles, and two long thin parts curved at the top. They are similar to tongs.

When:

- the baby's head struggles to get through the birth canal
- the woman is too tired to push
- the baby is distressed.

How: The top is fitted around the baby's head.
An **episiotomy** (small cut in the perineum) may be needed to allow more space for the forceps. Once the forceps are in place, the doctor will guide the baby's head out as the uterus contracts.

Ventouse

What: A type of suction cup

When:

- the baby's head struggles to get through the birth canal
- the woman is too tired to push
- the baby is distressed.

How: The top is fitted on the baby's head. As the uterus contracts, the doctor gently pulls to help the delivery.

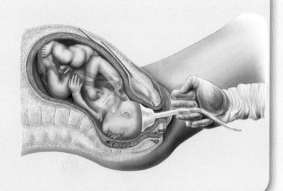

Revise it!

There are four methods of assisted birth. Create a flash card for each one. Write the name of the method on one side, and the details of when and how it is used on the other side. Check your knowledge regularly.

Remember it!

Forceps and **ventouse** both work in a similar way and are used when the baby is stuck in the birth canal.

Assisted birth 2 see p. 98

- How both surgical delivery methods are carried out
- Why an assisted birth may be necessary.

An episiotomy and a **caesarean section** (C-section) both require stitching. This is done after the delivery of the placenta (stage 3 of the birth).

Surgical intervention

Episiotomy

What: A small cut in the perineum (the area between the vagina and the anus).

When:

- more space is needed so the obstetrician can use forceps
- the baby's head needs help to get through the birth canal
- there is a risk of vaginal tearing – it's better to do a controlled cut to minimise the damage.

How: The cut is made during stage 2 and stitched up during stage 3.

C-section

What: A caesarean section is an operation in which the baby is delivered by cutting through the woman's uterus so the baby can be taken out.

When:

- the baby is in a breech position (feet down)
- in some multiple pregnancies
- the baby is lacking in oxygen and needs to be delivered immediately
- the woman experiences heavy bleeding or is not able to continue with labour for another medical reason
- the placenta is blocking the cervix preventing natural delivery (**placenta praevia**).

How: The woman is given an anaesthetic (either an epidural or general anaesthesia – meaning she would be unconscious). An elective C-section is planned if there are known problems. An emergency C-section is when things go wrong during natural labour.

Practise it!

1   Name *one* instrumental method of delivery.   **(1 mark)**
2   State *two* reasons why a woman may require a C-section.   **(2 marks)**

Remember it!

A C-section can be planned (elective) or unplanned (emergency).

Immediate postnatal checks 1 see p. 100

What you need to know

• What is checked immediately after birth
• Reasons for the postnatal checks.

There is a specific routine for examining a newborn. It is performed within the first minutes of the baby's life outside of the uterus.

APGAR score

The APGAR score is checked in the first minute of the baby's life and again five minutes later to look for progress. An APGAR score is out of 10.

Score	What it means for the baby
10–7	Healthy and well; no need for extra intervention
6–4	Needs to be observed; minor medical help required
3–0	Case of concern; needs the doctor's attention immediately

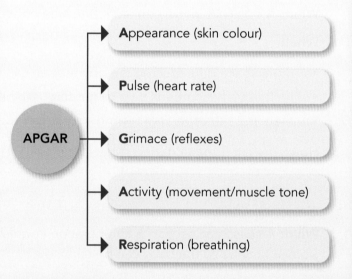

APGAR

- **A**ppearance (skin colour)
- **P**ulse (heart rate)
- **G**rimace (reflexes)
- **A**ctivity (movement/muscle tone)
- **R**espiration (breathing)

Birth weight

The baby is weighed at birth (and then at regular intervals) to ensure that there is a weight gain over time and to check that the baby is growing and developing normally. It also shows that the baby is feeding well.

Less than 2.5 kg (5.5 lb) – low
3.4–3.6 kg (7.5–8 lb) – average
More than 4 kg (8.8 lb) – high

Length

Length is measured from the top of the baby's head to the bottom of one of their heels. It is used to monitor the baby's growth.

Typically **between 50–53 cm** (average 51cm).

Head circumference

The measurement is taken around the baby's head. It is used to monitor brain growth. Typically, it is 35 cm (13 ¾ inches).

Revise it!

Know your numbers! Draw a simple picture of a newborn and annotate it to show the typical measurements: APGAR 10; weight 3.4 kg; length 51 cm; **head circumference** 35 cm.

Remember it!

The APGAR scale measures five elements: **A**ppearance, **P**ulse, **G**rimace, **A**ctivity, **R**espiration.

Immediate postnatal checks 2 see p. 100

- Skin examination
- The purpose of vernix and lanugo.

The APGAR scale is used to check the appearance (colour) of the newborn's skin. The midwife will also make a note of any birthmarks (moles, salmon patches, etc.) and residues of **vernix** and **lanugo**.

Skin examination

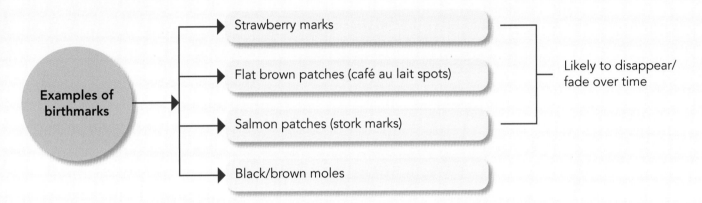

Vernix

Vernix is a greasy protective substance that covers the baby's skin in pregnancy and can be found on a newborn. The baby's skin will absorb it after birth. It shouldn't be washed off.

Functions:

- Lubricates the baby on its way through the birth canal.
- Keeps the baby's skin moist.
- Forms a protective barrier from bacteria.

Lanugo

Lanugo is very fine, soft hair that covers the baby's body. It is usually shed at the end of the pregnancy but can sometimes be seen on a newborn, especially if the baby was premature.

Functions:

- Keeps the baby's body at the right temperature.
- Binds the vernix to the skin, which helps to protect the skin.

Practise it!

1 List the *five* criteria checked during an APGAR examination. **(5 marks)**
2 Give *two* examples of birthmarks that could be found on a newborn's skin. **(2 marks)**

Remember it!

Vernix is the waxy protective substance, whilst lanugo is the fine hair that may be present on a newborn.

Additional postnatal examinations 1 see p. 102

What you need to know

- What checks are done within one to five days of birth
- Reasons for doing these checks.

A more detailed physical examination of a newborn happens between one and five days of life. These checks help determine the overall health of the baby but they are not vital.

Physical examination

Heart
A stethoscope is used to listen to the pulse. Unusual sounds, like a **heart murmur**, may suggest problems with the way the baby's heart pumps blood.

Eyes
It is natural for our eyes to reflect a red glow when exposed to light. A health professional uses a special torch to check a baby's eyes. If there is no red glow or the pupils appear white, this may suggest the baby has a **cataract** (an eye condition) that needs treatment.

Fontanelles
This is the soft spot on the baby's head. The skull bones are not fused at birth to allow the baby to pass through the birth canal. The health professional checks there is no bulging or sinking in the **fontanelles**.

Physical examination

Hips
Hips are checked to see if the joints are working properly. This is especially important if the baby was in a breech position as the joints might have dislocated (**hip dysplasia**).

Fingers
Fingers are checked for webbing (joined fingers). Also the palms would be checked for the number of creases – one could suggest Down's syndrome. Healthy children would have two creases.

Feet
Feet are checked to see if the baby has **club foot** (talipes) or if there is webbing between the toes.

Testicles
This applies to boys only. The health professional checks whether the testicles have descended and are correctly placed in the scrotum.

Revise it!

- Play 'Simon Says' to revise the different body parts that are checked during a postnatal examination. Say why this body part is examined.
- Alternatively, make up a new version of the song 'Head, Shoulders, Knees and Toes'.

Remember it!

- A cataract is an eye condition.
- Webbing refers to fingers and toes.
- Dysplasia affects the hips.

Additional postnatal examinations 2 see p. 102

What you need to know

- What a heel prick test is
- When and why it is done.

A heel prick test (also known as a 'newborn blood spot test') is offered by the NHS to all babies, usually on day 5. It helps with an early diagnosis of nine rare diseases. Parents can choose not to have it done.

Heel prick test

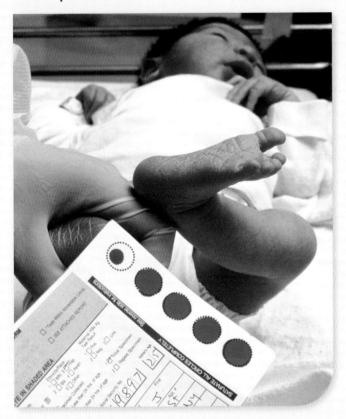

Why is it carried out?

It screens for nine rare but serious health conditions. By testing at this early stage, the baby is able to have early treatment which can help to prevent severe disability or death.

Examples of conditions that can be detected with the heel prick test

Sickle cell disease
affects the blood

Cystic fibrosis
affects the lungs and digestion

Congenital hypothyroidism
affects growth

Practise it!

1 Briefly explain *how* a newborn's eyes are tested as part of the physical examination. **(2 marks)**

2 Briefly explain *why* eyes are tested as part of the physical examination. **(2 marks)**

Remember it!

The heel prick test is usually done when a baby is five days old.

Postnatal care 1 see p. 103

What you need to know

- The role of the health visitor
- SIDS.

Postnatal care refers to the way the mother and her baby are looked after following labour. This involves both friends and professional care.

Health visitor

A health visitor is a registered nurse/midwife who works with families in the community. They take over from the midwife a few days after labour. Their role is:

- to monitor the baby's development (e.g. against the growth charts) and record it in their Personal Child Health Record (Red Book)
- to keep track of the baby's vaccination programme
- to assess the health and well-being of the baby and the new mother
- to offer information and support to new parents on aspects such as feeding, hygiene (including dental care) and safe sleeping (i.e. SIDS prevention).

Sudden Infant Death Syndrome (SIDS or 'cot death')

SIDS is when an apparently healthy baby dies without a clear medical explanation in the first six months of their life. When it happens, it is often because they stop breathing at night.

Prevention
• Place the baby on their back to sleep, never on their front.
• Have the cot in the parents' bedroom.
• **'Feet to foot'** position: the baby's feet should be touching the end of the cot.
• Keep the bedroom at a moderate temperature, i.e. 16–20 °C.
• Do not sleep with the baby in the same bed or fall asleep on the sofa/armchair with them.
• Do not place any extra objects in the baby's cot, e.g. teddy bears, pillows.
• Position the cot away from direct sunlight and radiators.
• Don't smoke in the house or use strong chemicals, including air fresheners.
• Keep rooms well ventilated.

Revise it!

Create a table of dos and don'ts for SIDS prevention. Put each of the statements above in the correct column. Look at your Student Book and add to your table.

Remember it!

The 'feet to foot' position is when you put the baby to sleep with its feet at the foot of the cot.

Postnatal care 2 see p. 103

- The support offered by the mother's partner, family and friends
- The purpose of the mother's six-week postnatal check with the GP.

A new mother's partner, friends and family can do a lot to help her. She will also need support from her GP to check her physical and mental health after the labour.

Partner, family and friends' support

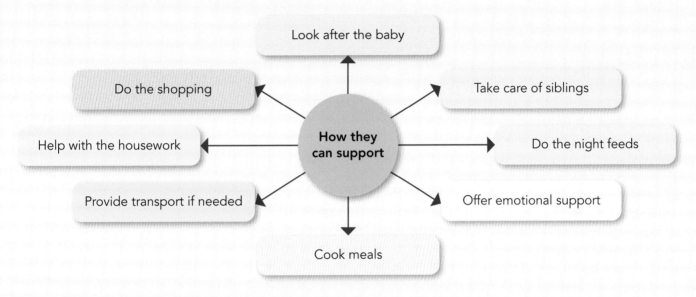

- Look after the baby
- Do the shopping
- Take care of siblings
- Help with the housework
- **How they can support**
- Do the night feeds
- Provide transport if needed
- Offer emotional support
- Cook meals

Mother's six-week postnatal check with the GP

This appointment is usually six to eight weeks after giving birth. The health checks include:

- mental health advice to prevent/diagnose possible postnatal depression
- checking the mother's physical health after labour including:
    - healing and stitches if the mother had a C-section or episiotomy
    - blood pressure
    - identifying any bleeding or discharge from the vagina
    - asking if periods have returned
    - weight check
- advice on contraception
- booking a smear test if the mother was due to have one during pregnancy.

Practise it!

1 Outline *two* things parents should do to help prevent SIDS. **(2 marks)**

2 Explain the support that can be given to a new mother by her partner, family and friends. **(4 marks)**

Remember it!

The six-week postnatal appointment with a GP is to monitor the mother's health and well-being, especially to check for postnatal depression, which is common after giving birth.

Developautal needs 1

Developmental needs 1 see p. 105

What you need to know

- The importance of each developmental need
- How these needs can be met.

Developmental needs are also known as 'conditions for development'. These are the elements of the child's environment that carers need to fulfil in order for the child to thrive and develop as expected.

Warmth

- Room temperature is suitable.
- Use a thermometer to check room and bathwater temperature.
- Carers should ensure a child has suitable indoor and outdoor clothing.
- A child should not play in the sun during the peak hours.
- A baby shouldn't be left in direct sun.

Feeding

- Both the quantity and the quality of food matter.
- A baby starts on milk feeds before moving on to **weaning**.
- From six months, feeding includes drinking liquids. Plenty of water should be offered to avoid dehydration (when your body hasn't had enough water).
- A poor diet can lead to many health problems including:
  - obesity (being overweight) if a child eats too many calories
  - malnutrition (poor physical health) if a child doesn't eat enough, or eats food that has little nutritional value
  - dental caries (tooth decay) if a child eats acidic and sweet food
  - anaemia (iron deficiency) caused by not eating enough food rich in iron.

Love and emotional security

- Emotional security is necessary for a child to establish their own sense of identity.
- Early emotional experiences influence a child's future relationship later. A lack of emotional security is very likely to have a negative impact on a child's behaviour, resulting in attention seeking, aggression, etc.
- Bonding or attachment is formed when: feeding, bathing, giving eye contact, through skin-to-skin contact, talking, reading and singing to a child, responding to their cries and comforting them.

Revise it!

Create flash cards from the important words in this topic: 'weaning', 'dehydration' and 'malnutrition'.

Remember it!

- The temperature of a room should be neither too hot nor too cold.
- Obesity and anaemia are two examples of dietary problems that can affect children.

Developmental needs 2 see p. 105

What you need to know

- The importance of each developmental need
- How these needs can be met.

The right conditions for development stimulate all aspects of a child's growth, for example sleep is needed for physical recovery as well as intellectual development.

Rest/sleep

- A newborn will sleep for up to 16 hours per day (with feeding breaks, of course!), while a five-year-old sleeps for around ten hours, including naps.
- The growth hormone is mainly released during a night's sleep.
- Rest is needed to consolidate learning and to allow the muscles to recover after intense activity – this is especially important in a child who has started walking.
- Every child needs a good sleep and rest routine, including quiet time between daily activities.
- The right environment for rest and sleep includes limited blue light exposure (no screen time before sleeping), optimal room temperature (16–20 °C), comfortable cot, etc.

Fresh air

- Indoor air often contains dust particles and smells from household chemicals.
- Being outdoors helps prevent pulmonary (lung-related) conditions.
- Fresh air means a child has access to sunlight, which boosts vitamin D production.

Exercise

- Exercise contributes to better sleep and reduces depression.
- Carers should ensure a child takes part in regular outdoors activities, e.g. playing in the garden, walking in the park or going to an outdoor playground.
- Exercise decreases the chance of obesity as calories are burnt. It also supports the development of a child's **gross motor skills** (using the large muscles, like legs).

Stimulation

- Daily stimulation creates new brain pathways allowing a child to learn.
- Carers should provide age-appropriate toys to create a stimulating environment.
- A child should be able to experience the world with all their senses: colours, noises, etc.
- Touching (e.g. cuddles) is particularly important for establishing emotional security.

Revise it!

Create a mind map. Write 'developmental needs' in the middle. Make a branch for each heading, and then add the bullet points.

Remember it!

- The optimal temperature for a room where a baby's sleeping is 16–20 °C.
- Controlling the temperature is one way to minimise the risk of SIDS.

Developmental needs 3 see p. 105

What you need to know

- The importance of each developmental need
- How these needs can be met.

A child's developmental needs change over time, for example the hygiene needs of a newborn are different to those of a five-year-old, but they both need to be cleaned.

Cleanliness/hygiene

- Babies and young children are more vulnerable to illness and infection than adults as their immune systems are still developing, so cleanliness and hygiene are very important.
- The cleaning routine for a newborn involves topping and tailing, nappy changes, and cleaning the naval area after the umbilical cord has fallen off.
- Always use baby toiletries as children's skin is more sensitive than adults' skin.
- Regularly wash clothes and bedding.
- Encourage children to look after their own hygiene, for example teach them to wash their hands and brush their teeth.
- Keep everywhere clean, especially areas like the kitchen where bacteria are common.
- Always **sterilise** feeding bottles.

Shelter/home

- A stable home environment influences a child's emotional and physical development.
- Carers need to ensure the physical safety of the home, for example using stair gates.
- Space for rest and play.
- Access to amenities, like childcare, parks and playgrounds.

Routine

- Regular daily patterns, especially when it comes to feeding, bath time and bedtime, are important. These things should occur at a similar time each day.
- Bathing and feeding routines are good for bonding.
- Routines help children feel less anxious and help parents plan their day better as they know what is going to happen and when.
- A feeding routine helps to make sure babies and children are fed regularly and are fed the right amount. It also allows carers to plan meals.
- A bath time and bedtime routine helps to calm babies and children before they go to sleep. A bath also provides an opportunity to check for any skin problems.

Revise it!

It's sensible to memorise two points from each of the developmental needs. Take a highlighter and choose two elements from each heading that you feel you can remember.

Remember it!

Baby hygiene is not only about keeping the child clean but it also includes activities like sterilising the feeding bottles and washing the bedding.

Revision Guide

Developmental needs 4 see p. 105

What you need to know

- The importance of each developmental need
- How these needs can be met.

Adults need to act as role models for the children in their care.

Socialisation and play

- **Socialisation** is learning how to form positive relationships with people and be part of the community.
- It includes learning the customs, values, manners and morals of a given social group.
- **Cooperative play** (playing with others) helps in developing socialisation, so it's important that a child has opportunities to mix with other children.
- Parents should include their child in family celebrations to help them feel a part of the extended family.
- Socialising stimulates intellectual and emotional development because a child learns to communicate with others and express themselves as an individual.

Opportunities for listening and talking

- A child needs to learn to communicate with others – it is important for their intellectual (**cognitive**), social and emotional development.
- If a child is misunderstood, it can affect their behaviour patterns, for example anger outbursts.
- Carers should encourage communication by reading and talking to a child.

Acceptable patterns of behaviour

- Young children need to learn the right social skills so that they will be ready for school.
- A child needs to have boundaries and expectations set for the sake of their safety (e.g. don't run into the road) and the safety of others (e.g. don't hit others).
- Carers should act as role models, for example not swearing.
- Carers should also use an effective praise and punishment system (e.g. a sticker chart or naughty stool).

Practise it!

1   List *four* developmental needs of a toddler. **(4 marks)**

2   Briefly explain the importance of appropriate stimulation for a child's development. **(2 marks)**

Remember it!

Parents are the best role models for the social development of their child.

Childhood illnesses 1 see p. 107

What you need to know

- Signs, symptoms and treatment of childhood illnesses.

There is a time lapse between when a child gets infected with a bacteria or a virus, and when the symptoms of an illness develop. This delay is called an incubation period.

Mumps

Signs and symptoms	Treatment
• Starts with a headache, joint pain and a high temperature • Later, the glands beneath the ears can swell up, making it difficult to chew and/or swallow	• Two weeks rest at home for the child to recover and to prevent the spread of the disease • Possibly give junior paracetamol to relieve the pain caused by swollen glands and ease the fever • Gently press a warm, wet compress or sponge on their swollen neck • Give plenty of fluids as the child is likely to be dehydrated from the fever

Measles

Signs and symptoms	Treatment
• Starts with flu-like symptoms (runny nose, sneezing and coughing, high temperature) • Sore red eyes, often sensitive to light • Small greyish-white spots inside the mouth • Later, a red rash appears, starting behind the ears, moving on to the face and spreading down	• A few days' rest at home for the child to recover and to prevent the spread of the disease • Possibly give junior paracetamol to relieve the pain and ease the fever • Clean their eyes with damp cotton wool and keep the room dark if possible • Give plenty of fluids as the child will likely be dehydrated due to fever

Revise it!

There are seven illnesses you need to know about for this topic. Create a factsheet for each one.

Remember it!

In addition to a fever, some diseases have specific symptoms, like greyish-white spots inside the mouth for measles or swollen neck glands for mumps.

Childhood illnesses 2 see p. 107

What you need to know

- Signs, symptoms and treatment of childhood illnesses.

Some illnesses are highly **contagious** and you must inform the child's GP about them. Mumps, measles and meningitis are all **notifiable diseases** and must be reported.

Meningitis

Signs and symptoms (a child may not develop all of these)	Treatment
• High temperature, headache, being sick and feeling drowsy • Stiff neck • A rash that doesn't fade when you roll a clear glass over it • Being sensitive to bright light • Possible seizures • Babies may be listless (limp) or refuse to feed	• Phone for an ambulance and pack a bag with the things the child will need in hospital • Antibiotics and fluids will usually be given in hospital • An oxygen mask may be applied • When home again, give the child plenty of rest and fluids. They may also need painkillers and anti-sickness medication

Tonsillitis

Signs and symptoms (a child may not develop all of these)	Treatment
• High temperature, headache, feeling sick and tired • Sore throat and cough • The neck glands can swell and a child may have white spots at the back of their throat	• A few days' rest at home • Give cool liquids or an ice lolly to ease throat pain • Give junior paracetamol to relieve the pain and decrease the fever

Revise it!

Write all the signs and symptoms of each illness on to strips of paper. Mix them up, then try to identify which symptom matches which illness.

Remember it!

Not every child will get a rash, but it is a very characteristic feature of meningitis. Press a glass against the child's skin to see whether the rash fades under pressure. If it doesn't, it's likely to be meningitis.

Childhood illnesses 3 see p. 107

What you need to know

- Signs, symptoms and treatment of childhood illnesses.

Young children often don't understand that they are ill and may not be able to communicate what their symptoms are. It is therefore very important that parents and carers are able recognise the signs and symptoms.

Chickenpox

Signs and symptoms	Treatment
• High temperature, pain in limbs and generally feeling unwell • Red, itchy spots can appear anywhere on the body; they fill with fluid, becoming blisters and eventually scabs.	• A few days' rest at home for the child to recover and to prevent the spread of the disease • Possibly give junior paracetamol to ease the pain or use cooling creams/gels to ease the itching • Bathe the child in cool water, patting the skin dry and dressing them in loose clothes • Cut the child's nails short or use anti-scratch mittens (or socks) to prevent them scratching the blisters.

Common cold

Signs and symptoms	Treatment
• Sore throat, blocked or runny nose, sneezing and coughing • Raised temperature, headache and muscle aches.	• A few days' rest at home for the child to recover and to prevent the spread of the disease • Possibly give junior paracetamol to relieve the pain and ease the fever • Give plenty of fluids as a child is likely to be dehydrated if they have a fever.

Revise it!

You may find it useful to apply visual stimuli to memorise the symptoms of various illnesses. Take a large sheet of plain paper and draw a simple human figure in the middle. Using different colours, mark the possible symptoms for each of the diseases; you can use the same colours to annotate possible treatment by drawing arrows around your figure.

Remember it!

For most illnesses, you can follow similar guidelines for recovery – keep the child at home, and give them plenty of rest and fluids to prevent dehydration.

Childhood illnesses 4 see p. 107

- Signs, symptoms and treatment of childhood illnesses.

Illnesses have different ways of transmission (the way someone can catch it). Most are spread via droplets (airborne diseases) when people sneeze, e.g. chickenpox, common cold or coronavirus.

Gastroenteritis

Signs and symptoms	Treatment
• Sudden, watery diarrhoea • Upset stomach, feeling sick and vomiting • A mild fever • Aches and pains.	• A few days' rest at home for the child to recover and to prevent the spread of the disease • Give plenty of fluids to avoid dehydration due to vomiting and diarrhoea • Give plenty of rest • Consult a pharmacist about over-the-counter medication for sickness and diarrhoea.

Key points to learn about childhood illnesses

- Fever is defined as having a body temperature that is 38°C or higher.
- Home remedies for reducing a fever in children include:
  - giving them a lukewarm (not too cold!) bath or sponging their body with cool water
  - applying a cool compress to their forehead
  - dressing them in loose clothes so they don't overheat
  - giving them plenty of fluids to drink.
- Keep an ill child at home to give them time to recover and to prevent spreading the illness further.
- Keep rooms ventilated and maintain good hygiene around the house to prevent the disease spreading.
- Never give children aspirin. They can be given junior paracetamol or ibuprofen, but parents and carers must always read the leaflet to check the correct dosage. This is often given as a liquid and measured in a ratio of millilitres to the body weight of the child.

Practise it!

1 Explain what is meant by a highly contagious disease. **(2 marks)**
2 Outline *two* symptoms of gastroenteritis. **(2 marks)**

Remember it!

Ways to reduce a fever at home include applying a cool compress to the child's forehead and sponging the child's body with lukewarm water.

Emergency medical help see p. 109

What you need to know

- Key signs and symptoms of when to seek emergency medical help.

It is not unusual for a child to feel unwell, but carers must be able to recognise when emergency medical help is required.

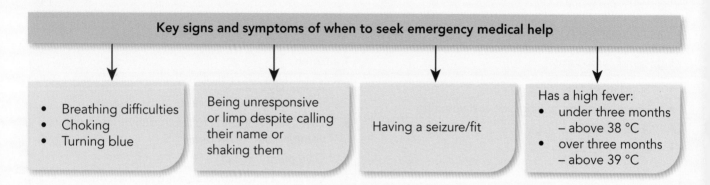

Key signs and symptoms of when to seek emergency medical help

- Breathing difficulties
- Choking
- Turning blue

Being unresponsive or limp despite calling their name or shaking them

Having a seizure/fit

Has a high fever:
- under three months – above 38 °C
- over three months – above 39 °C

What to do

- Call 999.
- If a child is unresponsive or limp, place them in the recovery position.
- If a child is choking, attempt back blows or abdominal thrusts.
- If a child has a seizure/fit, clear the area around them, remove any objects the child could hurt themselves on; place soft objects around them to prevent injury; once the seizure has stopped, place the child in the recovery position.

The recovery position

1 Lie the child on their back. Kneel by their side.
2 Place the child's arm closest to you at a right angle to the child, with their elbow bent to 90° and palm facing up.
3 Cross the other arm over the child's body, placing the back of their palm by their opposite cheek. Hold it in place with your hand.
4 With your other hand, grasp the far leg of the child above the knee and pull it up so that their knee is bent at a right angle.
5 Pull their leg towards you so that the child rolls to one side, facing you, with one of their hands under their face.
6 Check that the child's mouth is open and that they are breathing.
7 Stay with the child until the ambulance arrives.

Practise it!

1 Outline *two* signs that a child needs emergency medical attention. **(2 marks)**
2 Outline how a carer could help a child who is having an unexpected seizure. **(3 marks)**

Remember it!

A high fever means:

- 38°C or higher for a child under three months
- 39°C or higher for a child older than three months.

Meeting the needs of an ill child 1 see p. 110

What you need to know

- How the physical needs of an ill child can be met.

Physical needs are those that directly affect the way the body recovers. It includes food and medication.

Physical needs of an ill child

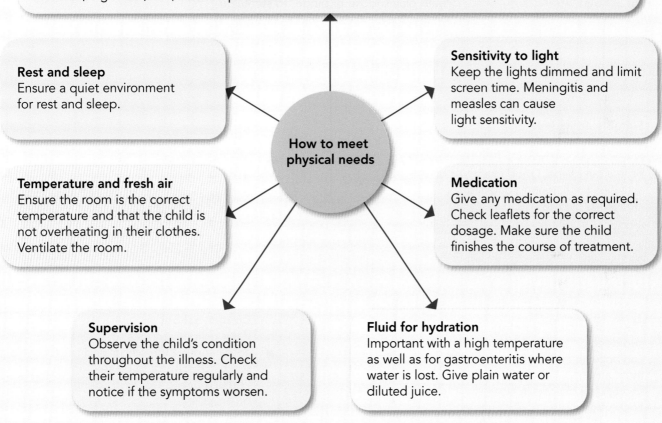

Food
Our bodies need energy to fight illness but some ill children lose their appetite or struggle with eating. Fruit has lots of vitamins which can help the immune system recover. For mumps, offer soup, or blend food to make it easier to swallow. For gastroenteritis, give plain food that won't upset the child's stomach, e.g. toast, rice, mashed potatoes.

Rest and sleep
Ensure a quiet environment for rest and sleep.

Temperature and fresh air
Ensure the room is the correct temperature and that the child is not overheating in their clothes. Ventilate the room.

How to meet physical needs

Sensitivity to light
Keep the lights dimmed and limit screen time. Meningitis and measles can cause light sensitivity.

Medication
Give any medication as required. Check leaflets for the correct dosage. Make sure the child finishes the course of treatment.

Supervision
Observe the child's condition throughout the illness. Check their temperature regularly and notice if the symptoms worsen.

Fluid for hydration
Important with a high temperature as well as for gastroenteritis where water is lost. Give plain water or diluted juice.

Revise it!

Some needs are specific to a particular illness. If you created factsheets for all the illnesses earlier, write the specific needs related to those illnesses on the back.

Remember it!

For measles and mumps, keep the lights dimmed as the child's eyes may be sore and/or sensitive to light.

Meeting the needs of an ill child 2 see p. 110

see p. 110

What you need to know

- How the intellectual needs of an ill child can be met.

Intellectual stimulation is important, especially if a child is absent from school. Gaps in knowledge can result in issues with **self-esteem** and problems once back at school.

Intellectual needs of an ill child

Target various skills
Activities should be focused on a variety of skills to compensate for the lack of schoolwork. To practise numeracy, a child could play sudoku or bingo; to stimulate literacy, they could be read to or they could write a story.

Suitable activities
It is important that activities are quiet and not too demanding as ill children may have a headache. Good examples of activities are colouring books or crossword puzzles.

Prevent boredom
Boredom can affect a child's intellectual and emotional state. Provide activities that are creative and inspiring for the child.

How to meet intellectual needs

Language exposure
Play educational TV programmes or audiobooks, so the child still has contact with spoken language. Talk to them and give them a chance to express themselves in words. Encourage texting/calling friends.

Contact school
If the child is school age, their carers could contact the school and ask for some schoolwork to be sent home. Perhaps online teaching could be arranged.

Revise it!

Make a list of games/activities that a child could be engaged with when staying at home/in hospital. For each activity, justify how it helps the intellectual development of a child, e.g. sudoku is great for numeracy. Put at least ten items on your list.

Remember it!

An ill child is likely to suffer from headaches and needs plenty of rest, so the activities chosen shouldn't be too demanding.

Meeting the needs of an ill child 3 see p. 110

What you need to know

- How the social and emotional needs of an ill child can be met.

A happy child is more likely to recover and feel less pain as the body can produce natural painkillers, i.e. endorphins. On the other hand, the body of a stressed child will release cortisol that slows down recovery.

Social needs of an ill child

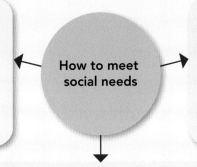

Support from friends/family
This could be done via phone (texting, calling) or online (FaceTime, WhatsApp, Teams, etc.). If a child is not contagious, then visitors can be invited over.

How to meet social needs

Manners/behaviour
Continue enforcing high expectations for positive behaviour and manners, e.g. reminding the child to use 'please' and 'thank you'; reward good behaviour and talk with the child about any behaviour incidents you are not happy with.

Social activities
Social skills can be learnt from reading books with moral lessons. Role playing nurse and patient could help a child understand the roles of health professionals.

Emotional needs of an ill child

Be honest
A child may feel guilty that they are ill. Perhaps they think they brought the illness on themselves. They may not fully understand how serious their condition is. Reassure them about the situation.

How to meet emotional needs

Skin-to-skin contact
Touch is very powerful. It provides skin stimulation and emotional comfort. Cuddle or stroke an ill child.

Provide comforters
This could be a favourite blanket, teddy bear or pictures of their favourite cartoon characters.

Quality time/attention
Make sure the child feels loved by giving them your time and attention. Sit with them and spend time talking and listening.

Practise it!

1. Outline *two* ways carers can meet the intellectual needs of an ill child. **(2 marks)**
2. Explain why it is important to meet the emotional needs of an ill child. **(2 marks)**

Remember it!

Comforters are objects that a child has a positive emotional attachment to, e.g. a favourite teddy bear.

Hazard prevention 1 see p. 112

What you need to know

- The meaning of the term '**hazard**'
- Recognise common hazards and the ways of preventing them.

A hazard is something that may cause you or others harm. There are many hazards in a child's environment, so it is important to know the risks.

Types of hazards

- Physical hazards, like broken objects or slippery floors
- Biological hazards, like bacteria, mould or animal faeces (poo)
- Fire hazards, like faulty electrical equipment
- Security hazards, like an unlocked gate

Why are children more likely to suffer accidents?

- They're often unaware of hazards and their consequences.
- They're short, so they may not notice the hazard, and they may not be noticed by others, e.g. car drivers.
- Their muscle coordination is still developing, so they're more clumsy and may be unsteady when walking.
- Their carers may be untrained or there may be a lack of supervision.

Kitchen

Hazards	Prevention
<ul><li>Hot objects: burns, scalds</li><li>Sharp objects: cuts</li><li>Kitchen chemicals: poisoning, skin irritation</li><li>Food contamination: **food poisoning**</li><li>Oil and grease: fire</li><li>Spilled liquids: slips, falls, bacteria growth</li><li>Blinds: strangulation with cord</li><li>Objects falling from high shelves: bruises</li></ul>	<ul><li>Always supervise a child in the kitchen.</li><li>Install a cooker guard.</li><li>Turn pan handles inwards towards the wall.</li><li>Use cordless kettles or keep the flex well out of reach.</li><li>Keep knives out of reach.</li><li>Store chemicals in a locked cupboard, out of reach.</li><li>Follow food hygiene advice.</li><li>Clear up any spillages straight away.</li><li>Keep a fire blanket or extinguisher in the kitchen.</li></ul>

Revise it!

Expand the examples of types of hazards. Add three more examples to each one.

Remember it!

A hazard is anything that can lead to someone getting hurt. Sometimes is it an object (e.g. a sharp knife), sometimes it's an action (e.g. leaving a stairgate open).

Hazard prevention 2 see p. 112

- Recognise common hazards and the ways of preventing them.

A **risk assessment** is a document that, by law, an establishment like a nursery or school must have to explain the dangers and state how staff can minimise the risks.

Bathroom

Hazards	Prevention
• Hot water: scalds • Bath: drowning • Cleaning chemicals: poisoning, skin irritation • Spilled liquids: slips, falls, bacteria growth • Toilet: bacteria contamination	• Fill a bath with cold water first. • Lower the temperature of the boiler. • Supervise a child in a bath. • Keep chemicals safely locked away. • Clean any spillages straight away. • Regularly clean the toilet and surfaces. • Teach personal hygiene.

Stairs

Hazards	Prevention
• Stairs: trips and falls • Stair balustrade: a body part can get stuck • Lack of light: trips and falls • Wooden stairs: cuts and bruises from falls • Worn carpets: slips and falls	• Put stairgates at the bottom and top. • Teach a child how to use stairs safely. • Install child-height hand rails. • Make sure stairs are well lit. • Cover the stairs with carpet. • Check the condition of the stairs regularly.

Outdoors

Hazards	Prevention
• Animal faeces: contamination, poisoning • Poisonous plants/berries/mushrooms: poisoning • Insects: bites, stings • Broken gates/fences: security risk • Garden equipment: possible serious injury • Play equipment: cuts and bruises	• Clear up any animal faeces straight away. • Remove weeds and mushrooms. • Be mindful of insects, e.g. bee hives. • Repair any broken gates/fence panels. • Keep garden equipment stored securely. • Inspect play equipment regularly.

Revise it!

Create a risk assessment, pointing out some possible dangers in your own home and suggest ways of making it a safer place.

Remember it!

Every public institution must have a risk assessment. A nursery would be breaking the law if they didn't have one.

Hazard prevention 3 see p. 112

What you need to know

- Recognise common hazards and ways of preventing them.

Roads are dangerous places. Car drivers may not see a small child running into the street. There is also a delay between when a driver presses the brake pedal and when the car actually stops (breaking distance).

Road safety

Ways to prevent road traffic **accidents**:

- Teach children the Green Cross Code.
- Use reins when walking with a young child.
- Make sure a child is holding your hand when close to a busy road.
- Always let the child walk on the inside of the pavement, further away from the road.
- Make the child wear high-visibility clothes, so that they can be easily seen by drivers.
- If playing ball games, ensure the chosen play area is far from moving traffic.
- When travelling by car, make sure the child locks are engaged.
- Use an age-specific car seat when the child is with you in a car (it is a legal requirement for children until they reach 12 years of age or become taller than 135 cm – whichever comes first).
- If using the rear-facing car seat, deactivate the passenger airbag.

Green Cross Code

1   **THINK!** – find the safe place to cross; do not cross on the bends or around trees obstructing the view
2   **STOP!** – stand on the pavement near the kerb but keeping distance from the road
3   **LOOK and LISTEN!** – check if you can see any oncoming traffic; listen to hear for any cars coming
4   **WAIT!** – patiently wait for any cars to pass; wait until it is safe to cross
5   **LOOK and LISTEN (again)!** – keep monitoring the traffic once you've started crossing
6   **ARRIVE ALIVE!** – do not run (you may fall over) and do not cross diagonally

Practise it!

1   Outline *two* hazards that could be found in a garden.   **(2 marks)**
2   Outline *two* ways in which carers can make a garden safer.   **(2 marks)**

Remember it!

Road supervision includes using reins, holding the child's hand and making sure they walk on the inside of the pavement.

Safety labels see p. 114

What you need to know

- The meaning of each safety label
- Examples of products on which each label can be found.

All safety labels must be securely and permanently attached (or imprinted) on to the item sold. With clothing, the label should still be visible after washing.

Safety labels

The British Standards Institution (BSI) Kitemark is a quality mark that shows a product meets the relevant and appropriate British, European or other internationally recognised standards for quality, safety, performance and trust. Examples of products that are likely to have the BSI Kitemark are: bike helmets, bottle sterilisers, baby car seats, electronic gadgets.

The Lion Mark was developed by the British Toy and Hobby Association (BTHA) which supplies around 90% of toys sold in the UK. It was developed in 1988 to act as a recognisable consumer symbol denoting safety and quality of a toy, as well as its educational value. Products which display the Lion Mark include soft toys and board games.

The Age Warning symbol warns adults that items are not suitable for a child under three years of age (36 months). This is usually because the item has small parts that could be a choking hazard. Examples of products with the Age Warning symbol are: teddy bears, board games, LEGO® bricks.

The CE symbol must be used on products that are for sale in the EU. They must meet the required safety standards. As the UK has left the EU, the British equivalent of the CE mark is the UKCA. Examples of products that display the CE/UKCA symbol are: teddy bears, feeding bottles, stairgates.

Due to the potential fire risk, children's nightwear must comply with flammability requirements, meaning that it must be difficult for it to catch fire and if it does, it must not burn quickly. Other than children's nightwear, it would be also found on mattresses and bedding. You will recognise this label by the wording: low flammability, keep away from fire or compliant with BS 5722 standards.

Practise it!

1. Give *two* specific products that should have a BSI Kitemark symbol on them. **(2 marks)**
2. Name *one* safety label that would be found on a feeding bottle. **(1 mark)**

Remember it!

The Age Warning label refers to the age of three years and below (not three months!).

Pre-conception health 1 and 2 see p. 20–21

1 Explain what is meant by the term 'pre-conception health'. **(2 marks)**

....

....

....

2 Zain and Zara are planning their first pregnancy. Zain sees that Zara has stopped drinking alcohol and started eating much more healthily. He tells his friend, 'Pregnancy is the woman's effort, so I don't have to prepare much.'

   (a) Explain why Zain should also consider pre-conception health as a father-to-be. **(2 marks)**

   ....

   ....

   ....

   (b) Identify *two* factors Zain could consider as part of his pre-conception health. **(2 marks)**

   1 ....

   2 ....

3 Age is one of the most important factors for pre-conception health.
   Read the statements below. Which ones apply to women and which ones apply to men? Put a tick (✓) in the correct column. **(3 marks)**

	Women	Men
(a) Are affected by the menopause.	☐	☐
(b) Stay fertile all their adult life.	☐	☐
(c) Have an increased risk of conceiving a baby with Down's syndrome when older.	☐	☐

4 Using your knowledge of pre-conception health and the statements in question 3, explain the importance of age in deciding when to start a family. **(4 marks)**

....

....

....

....

....

....

Folic acid and immunisations see p. 22

1 Identify *two* natural sources of folic acid in food. **(2 marks)**

1 ....

....

2 ....

....

2 Read and circle ◯. Are the statements about folic acid *true* or *false*? **(4 marks)**

(a) Folic acid is needed for the production of blood cells. True / False

(b) Folic acid minimises the risk of a baby having Down's syndrome. True / False

(c) Folic acid can be obtained from recommended vitamin supplements. True / False

(d) Folic acid is important for the formation of the embryo's neural tube. True / False

3 Gurveen is thinking of having a baby. Her GP tells her about the importance of having up-to-date immunisations. The GP looks at Gurveen's medical records and suggests that she should have the flu vaccination. Imagine you are Gurveen's doctor. Explain to Gurveen why it is important for her to have this vaccine. **(3 marks)**

....

....

....

....

....

....

4 Complete the sentences using the words in the box.

> flu   rubella   whooping cough

(a) The .... vaccine can help prevent pneumonia in newborns.

(b) .... is particularly dangerous if caught whilst pregnant.

(c) A pregnant woman has a higher risk of developing complications if she catches

.... **(3 marks)**

Barrier methods of contraception see p. 23

1   John teaches his son, Freddie, about contraception. He says that a male condom
    is easy to use and very effective. Explain to Freddie how a male condom works
    to prevent pregnancy.   **(3 marks)**

    ....

    ....

    ....

    ....

    ....

    ....

2   Match the barrier methods of contraception with their typical level of protection. **(3 marks)**

    | diaphragm/cap   female condom   male condom |

    92–96% ....   98% ....   95% ....

3   Outline *one* advantage of using a diaphragm as a method of contraception.   **(1 mark)**

    ....

    ....

4   Not every couple likes to use condoms. Outline *two* possible reasons why
    someone may decide not to choose condoms as a method of contraception.   **(2 marks)**

    ....

    ....

5   Read and tick (✓). Which of the couples below would be most likely to use
    a barrier method of contraception? Choose *two*.   **(2 marks)**

    (a) A new couple who want to prevent pregnancy and protect themselves from STIs   ☐

    (b) A couple where the woman cannot take hormones   ☐

    (c) A couple who value uninterrupted sex   ☐

    (d) A well-established couple looking for long-term protection from pregnancy   ☐

Non-barrier methods of contraception 1 and 2 see p. 24–25

1   A synthetic version of the hormone progesterone is commonly used in contraceptive pills, implants and injections. Explain the role of progesterone in preventing pregnancy.   **(2 marks)**

....

....

....

2   Draw a line to match each method of contraception with the correct feature.   **(7 marks)**

(a) Contraceptive implant	**(i)** One pill taken at the same time each day; releases progesterone only.
(b) Combined pill	**(ii)** Inserted into the uterus; can cause side effects, such as acne or mood swings.
(c) IUD	**(iii)** Lasts for 8–13 weeks; fertility may not come back immediately after stopping using it.
(d) Contraceptive injection	**(iv)** Used after unprotected sex; not recommended as a regular contraceptive method.
(e) POP	**(v)** Uses two synthetic hormones (progesterone and oestrogen).
(f) IUS	**(vi)** Made of copper; the longest lasting method of contraception.
(g) Emergency contraceptive pill	**(vii)** Inserted under the skin; lasts for three years.

3   Suggest a suitable non-barrier method of contraception for each of these couples. There is more than one correct answer in some cases, but you are only required to give *one* suggestion.   **(4 marks)**

(a) Magda and Maciej already have three children and do not want to have any more. Their youngest daughter is only six weeks old. Magda is breastfeeding, so choose a method of contraception which takes that into account.

....

(b) Ciara and Ian are engaged. They don't want children just yet, but would like to start trying for a baby after their wedding in two years' time. Ciara cannot take any oestrogen-based pills.

....

(c) Francesca and Luke have been dating for a while. They always use a condom but last night it split. Francesca needs a solution that works after intercourse has taken place.

....

(d) Aiko is in a stable relationship with Yoshi. She has very painful periods and would like a method of contraception that will prevent pregnancy and make her periods lighter and less painful.

....

4 IUDs (intrauterine devices) and IUSs (intrauterine systems) are two popular methods of contraception. Discuss the strengths and weaknesses of using these two types of contraception. **(6 marks)**

....

....

....

....

....

....

....

....

Natural family planning see p. 26

1   Natural family planning is when a woman is aware of her cycle and plans to have sex on the days in which she is less fertile (and therefore less likely to get pregnant) to avoid unwanted pregnancy. Identify the *three* methods of natural family planning.   **(3 marks)**

    1   ....

    2   ....

    3   ....

2   Read and circle ⃝ the correct words to complete the sentences.   **(3 marks)**

    (a)   As part of natural family planning, a woman keeps a log of her **periods / weight**.

    (b)   She learns how to recognise her **implantation / ovulation** day and **has / avoids** sex at that time if she does not wish to become pregnant.

    (c)   If used correctly, the method is up to **95% / 99%** effective in preventing pregnancy.

3   Read and circle ⃝. Are the statements about natural family planning *true* or *false*?   **(5 marks)**

    (a)   Natural family planning is accepted by all religions.   True / False

    (b)   Natural family planning protects against STIs.   True / False

    (c)   You need to consult your doctor before starting natural family planning.   True / False

    (d)   A woman must have regular menstrual cycles for natural family planning to work correctly.   True / False

    (e)   Couples who do not wish to have children can only have unprotected sex on less fertile days.   True / False

4   Sharan wants to find out more about natural family planning. Explain how she could use *two* of the natural family planning methods to prevent unwanted pregnancy.   **(6 marks)**

    (a)   ....

          ....

          ....

          ....

    (b)   ....

          ....

          ....

          ....

Female reproductive system 1 see p. 27

1 Complete the words with the missing letters. **(5 marks)**

    (a) va _ _ _ a

    (b) oe _ _ _ _ gen

    (c) ute _ _ _

    (d) fa _ _ _ pi _ _ tube

    (e) c _ _ v _ _

2 Label the diagram. **(3 marks)**

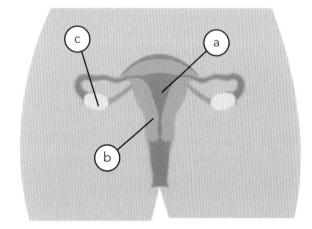

    (a) ....

    (b) ....

    (c) ....

3 Read the definitions. Write the word next to the correct definition. **(4 marks)**

> **womb**   **vagina**   **fallopian tubes**   **cervix**

    (a) They connect the ovaries to the uterus. Fertilisation happens here. ....

    (b) It is also called 'the neck of the uterus'. It protects the uterus and produces mucus that

        lubricates the vagina. ....

    (c) This is a muscular canal. It has important functions during menstrual periods,

        sexual intercourse and labour. ....

    (d) A hollow, pear-shaped organ that holds the unborn baby. If an egg is not fertilised,

        it sheds its lining every month as a menstrual period. ....

4 Following the example definitions in question 3, write a definition for 'ovary'. **(2 marks)**

....

....

....

Female reproductive system 2 see p. 28

1 Label the menstrual cycle diagram below (a–b). The first letter of the missing words has been given to help you. Then circle ◯ the correct option to show the most fertile and least fertile days in the female cycle (i–iii). **(5 marks)**

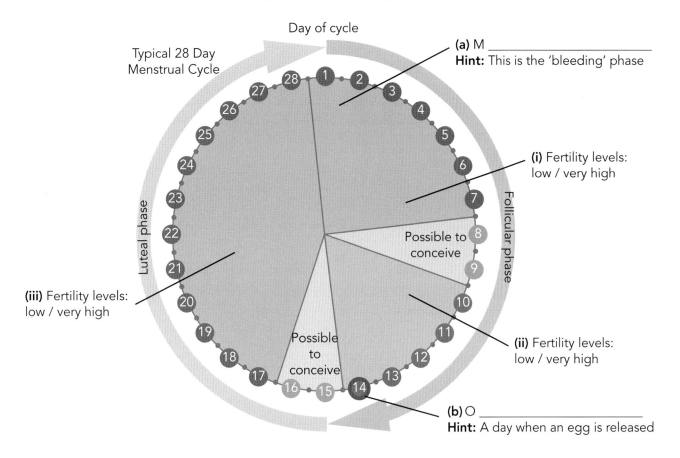

Day of cycle

Typical 28 Day Menstrual Cycle

(a) M _____
Hint: This is the 'bleeding' phase

(i) Fertility levels: low / very high

Follicular phase

Possible to conceive

Luteal phase

(iii) Fertility levels: low / very high

Possible to conceive

(ii) Fertility levels: low / very high

(b) O _____
Hint: A day when an egg is released

2 Number the stages of the menstrual cycle in the correct order. One has been done for you. **(4 marks)**

(a) Ovulation (i.e. an egg is released from an ovary) ....

(b) The lining of the uterus breaks down resulting in a menstrual period. ....*1*.........

(c) The uterus lining remains thick, ready to receive a fertilised egg. ....

(d) The uterus lining gradually thickens again in preparation for ovulation. ....

(e) If an egg is not fertilised, the uterus lining prepares to shed again. ....

3 Read and circle ◯. Are the statements *true* or *false*? **(4 marks)**

(a) The medical name for a woman's period is 'menstruation'. True / False

(b) Ovulation happens on the seventh day of a typical menstrual cycle. True / False

(c) A woman's fertility levels are lowest on ovulation day. True / False

(d) Normally, a woman produces two eggs each month, one from each ovary. True / False

Male reproductive system see p. 29

1 Complete the words with the missing letters. **(4 marks)**

(a) ep _ d _ d _ mis

(b) vas d _ _ _ _ _ _ s

(c) ur _ _ _ ra

(d) s _ _ _ nal ve _ _ _ _ _ _ _

2 Label the diagram. **(3 marks)**

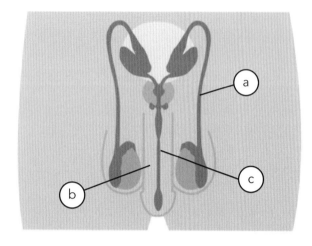

(a) ....

(b) ....

(c) ....

3 Read the definitions below. Write the word next to the correct definition. **(4 marks)**

> epididymis   seminal vesicle   testes   penis

(a) They are behind the penis. They produce sperm and testosterone. ....

(b) A muscular tube that can penetrate the vagina when erect during sexual intercourse.

It also has a role in urination. ....

(c) They produce a nutritious fluid that combines with sperm to create semen.

....

(d) A long, coiled tube where sperm mature before being transported to the vas deferens.

....

4 Following the example definitions in question 3, write a definition for 'urethra'. **(2 marks)**

Urethra: ....

....

....

How reproduction takes place 1 and 2 see p. 30–31

1   Complete the sentences in this text about how fertilisation takes place.   **(5 marks)**

A couple should aim to have sex around .... day to maximise their chances of

successful conception. The man places his erect penis into the woman's vagina. During ejaculation

the semen, which contains the sperm, travels to the ...., where fertilisation

takes place. The fertilised egg travels to the .... where it burrows into the

lining. This process is called ...., and the new cell formation is referred

to as an ....

2   Identify the sex of a baby if an egg is fertilised by a Y sperm cell.   **(1 mark)**

    ....

3   Read and circle ◯. Are the statements *true* or *false*?   **(4 marks)**

    (a) In a healthy pregnancy, a fertilised egg implants itself in the fallopian tube.   True / False

    (b) Implantation takes place six to ten days after fertilisation.   True / False

    (c) An implanted fertilised egg is called an embryo.   True / False

    (d) The female egg determines the sex of a baby.   True / False

4   Annotate the diagram to show where fertilisation takes place and where
    implantation happens.   **(2 marks)**

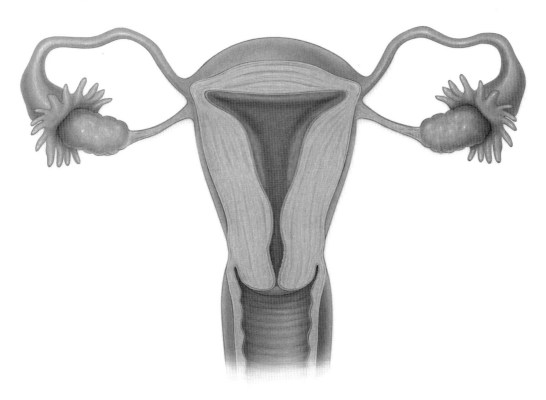

Development of the embryo and foetus see p. 32

1 Complete the sentences using the words in the box. **(5 marks)**

| organ | liquid | sac | tube | uterus |

(a) Amniotic fluid is a transparent .... inside a ....
that surrounds the embryo/foetus.

(b) The umbilical cord is a .... that connects the embryo/foetus to the
pregnant woman's placenta.

(c) The placenta is a temporary .... that supports the embryo/foetus.

It is attached to the wall of the ....

2 Match the structures (a–c) to their functions (i–vi). Some structures have more
than one function. **(6 marks)**

(a) Amniotic fluid

(b) Umbilical cord

(c) Placenta

(i) Transfers nutrients to the embryo/foetus.

(ii) Releases hormones that are needed in pregnancy.

(iii) Helps to maintain the temperature in the womb.

(iv) Acts as a cushion to protect the embryo/foetus in the belly.

(v) Transfers waste products from the baby to the placenta
for filtration.

(vi) Supplies nutrients that will be transferred to the
unborn baby.

3 In which week of pregnancy does the embryo turn into a foetus? **(1 mark)**

....

4 Complete the sentences using words in the box. **(7 marks)**

| alcohol | blood | carbon dioxide | food nutrients | oxygen | urea | water |

(a) These elements are transferred from a pregnant woman to her baby:

....

(b) These are transferred from the baby to the pregnant woman: ....

....

(c) This isn't transferred: ....

Multiple pregnancies see p. 33

1 Read statements a–e. Which apply to identical twins and which apply to non-identical twins? Put a tick (✓) in the correct column. **(5 marks)**

	Identical twins	Non-identical twins
(a) They do not look alike.	☐	☑
(b) They are always the same sex.	☑	☐
(c) They are created from two different eggs.	☐	☑
(d) They share the same placenta.	☑	☐
(e) They are fertilised by the same single sperm.	☑	☐

2 Read and circle ◯ the correct words to complete the sentences. **(4 marks)**

(a) Multiple pregnancies can lead to (premature) / delayed labour.

(b) It is (more) / less likely that a woman will have a C-section with a multiple pregnancy.

(c) Multiple pregnancies decrease / (increase) the risk of miscarriage.

(d) Babies born from multiple pregnancies have a lower / (higher) chance of being born with abnormalities.

3 Jenny is at her first ultrasound scan and has just found out she is pregnant with non-identical (fraternal) twins.

(a) Explain how non–identical twins are formed. **(2 marks)**

....

....

....

....

(b) Explain how a sonographer would recognise non-identical twins on an ultrasound scan. **(1 mark)**

....

....

Signs and symptoms of pregnancy see p. 34

1   Read the scenario. Niamh is talking to her GP. Identify *three* main signs and
    symptoms of early pregnancy that Niamh is experiencing.   **(3 marks)**

    'I feel a bit weird these days. I am sleepy all the time and I seem to lack the energy I had
    just a month ago. It's not helping that I also feel nauseous. Yesterday, I even vomited
    at work. My period is late. I did have a small amount of bleeding three days ago but it
    didn't last as long as it usually does.'

    1   ....

    2   ....

    3   ....

2   One of the signs not mentioned by Niamh is changes to her breasts. Outline *two*
    changes that can be observed in women's breasts that might indicate pregnancy.   **(2 marks)**

    1   ....

        ....

    2   ....

        ....

3   Read and circle ◯. Are the statements *true* or *false*?   **(4 marks)**

    (a) Morning sickness can happen at any time of the day.   True / False

    (b) Early pregnancy symptoms are caused by an increase in testosterone.   True / False

    (c) Minor blood spotting is typical in the first two weeks of pregnancy.   True / False

    (d) Frequent urination only affects women in the first month of pregnancy.   True / False

4   There are *two* false statements in question 3. Correct the false statements.   **(2 marks)**

    ....

    ....

    ....

    ....

    ....

Workbook

Professionals involved in antenatal care see p. 35

1   Define the term 'antenatal care'.   (1 mark)

....

....

2   Give *two* examples of antenatal care.   (2 marks)

1   ....

2   ....

3   Match the health professionals involved in antenatal care (a–c) with
    the definitions (i–iii).   (3 marks)

(a) GP   (i)   A specialist trained to monitor normal
                                      pregnancies and deliver most babies

(b) Midwife   (ii) A doctor trained to deal with pregnancy
                                      complications and difficult labours

(c) Obstetrician   (iii) A doctor trained in general medicine who
                                      can make specialist referrals

4   Read statements a–d and tick (✓). Which statement is typical for the role of a
    general practitioner (GP), midwife (MW) or obstetrician (OBS)?   (4 marks)

	GP	MW	OBS
(a) This person is qualified to perform C-sections.	☐	☐	☐
(b) This person would be consulted to find out more about the pregnant woman's pre-existing medical conditions.	☐	☐	☐
(c) This person arranges screening tests.	☐	☐	☐
(d) This person delivers antenatal (parenting) classes.	☐	☐	☐

5   Lydia wants to become a midwife when she's older. Explain the role of a midwife
    in supporting a pregnant woman throughout the pregnancy to help Lydia
    understand what the job involves.   (3 marks)

....

....

....

....

....

Antenatal clinic appointments 1 and 2 see p. 36–37

1   Oksana is attending her first antenatal appointment. State why the midwife asks
    Oksana what the first day of her last period was.   **(1 mark)**

    ....

    ....

2   Oksana's midwife explains that she needs to take a blood sample and send it to
    the lab for further analysis. Explain *two* reasons for blood tests in pregnancy.   **(4 marks)**

    Reason 1: ....

    ....

    ....

    Reason 2: ....

    ....

    ....

3   Read and circle ◯ the correct words or numbers to complete the sentences.   **(4 marks)**

    (a) A healthy unborn baby's heartbeat is **80–100 / 110–160** beats per minute.

    (b) Pre-eclampsia can be indicated by **low / high** blood pressure.

    (c) Anaemia is diagnosed when iron levels in the pregnant woman's blood are too **low / high**.

    (d) Sudden weight **loss / gain** in pregnancy can be a sign of pre-eclampsia or diabetes.

4   Read and tick (✓). Which of the tests and checks help to identify the following
    health problems?   **(8 marks)**

    Tip: you need to put eight ticks – the same as the number of marks for
    this question.

	Blood sample	Urine test	Uterus exam	Blood pressure
(a) Diagnose gestational diabetes				
(b) Determine baby's position in the uterus				
(c) Identify the pregnant woman's rhesus factor and blood group				
(d) Diagnose pre-eclampsia				
(e) Diagnose anaemia				

Screening and diagnostic tests see p. 38–39

1 Read and tick (✓). Which tests are screening tests and which are diagnostic tests? **(5 marks)**

	Screening	Diagnostic
(a) Nuchal fold translucency scan	☐	☐
(b) Triple test	☐	☐
(c) Amniocentesis	☐	☐
(d) Dating scan	☐	☐
(e) CVS	☐	☐

2 Read the descriptions. For each one, state which test is being described. **(5 marks)**

(a) This scan is offered later in the pregnancy. It checks the baby's growth and checks for specific abnormalities, like cleft palate or serious cardiac problems.

....

(b) This blood test is not offered by the NHS but parents may decide to do it privately. It can be done very early in the pregnancy and can indicate possible genetic mutations or chromosomal abnormalities in an unborn baby.

....

(c) This test is an invasive method that involves taking a sample of amniotic fluid. It is offered between the weeks 15 and 20. It can lead to a diagnosis of Down's syndrome or cystic fibrosis. It isn't offered to everyone as it has a small risk of miscarriage.

....

(d) This scan is likely to be the first scan a pregnant woman has. It shows whether she is pregnant with a single child, twins or more. It is also helpful in confirming the estimated due date.

....

(e) This test is often combined with the first scan. The sonographer measures the thickness of the foetus' neck fold to check for Down's syndrome.

....

3 The text describes the differences between amniocentesis and chorionic villus sampling. Complete the sentences using the words and numbers in the box. **(8 marks)**

> 11   amniocentesis   14   CVS   15   cystic fibrosis   20
> Down's syndrome   needle   vagina

.... is usually done between week .... and week

.... of pregnancy, whilst .... is offered later, i.e. between

week .... and week .... They both help to diagnose serious

conditions, such as .... and .... The main difference is

that in CVS a sample is obtained through the .... whilst in amniocentesis a

.... is inserted into the uterus. It is monitored by an ultrasound device.

4 Judith has been informed that her child will be born with an open spina bifida.

(a) Describe to Judith what open spina bifida is. **(2 marks)**

....

....

....

(b) Name *one* diagnostic test that would be used to confirm open spina bifida. **(1 mark)**

....

5 Other than open spina bifida, name *two* more conditions that could be diagnosed by antenatal screening and/or diagnostic tests. **(2 marks)**

(a) ....

(b) ....

6 Write the full names of these tests. **(3 marks)**

(a) CVS ....

(b) NFT scan ....

(c) NIPT ....

Antenatal (parenting) classes 1–3 see p. 40–42

1   Magda is trying to convince Maciej to join her at the antenatal classes she is
    already attending. Explain *two* benefits for Maciej if he attended the classes
    as a father/birthing partner.   **(4 marks)**

    ....

    ....

    ....

    ....

    ....

    ....

    ....

2   From the food items below, choose *two* sets that Magda should be avoiding
    or limiting in pregnancy. Explain why those items should be avoided.   **(4 marks)**

(a) raw shellfish, too much oily fish, too much tuna	**(b)** croissants and bread
(c) wine and beer	**(d)** hotdogs and French fries

    Item set: .... Reason for avoiding: ....

    ....

    Item set: .... Reason for avoiding: ....

    ....

3   Other than dietary requirements, outline *two* more things Magda will have
    learnt at the antenatal classes about having a healthy lifestyle in pregnancy.   **(2 marks)**

    1   ....

    ....

    2   ....

    ....

4 Draw lines to match the words with the correct definition. **(7 marks)**

(a) Salmonella

(b) Colostrum

(c) Topping and tailing

(d) Toxoplasmosis

(e) Mastitis

(f) Listeria

(i) A type of bacteria that may be present in unpasteurised dairy foods

(ii) A nutritious substance full of antibodies that is passed from mother to baby by breastfeeding

(iii) A way of cleaning a baby using warm water and cotton wool

(iv) A type of bacteria that can be found in raw eggs

(v) Painful breast inflammation that may cause problems when breastfeeding

(vi) A disease caused by a parasite found in undercooked meat or unwashed fruit and vegetables

5 An important part of antenatal classes is to teach future parents how to feed their baby.

(a) Outline *one* benefit of early breastfeeding for the baby. **(1 mark)**

....

....

....

(b) Outline *one* benefit of early breastfeeding for the mother. **(1 mark)**

....

....

....

(c) Outline *two* problems that may prevent the mother from successfully breastfeeding. **(2 marks)**

1 ....

....

....

2 ....

....

....

Choices available for delivery see p. 43–44

1   Read and tick (✓). Which statements apply to hospital births and which apply to home births? **(5 marks)**

	Hospital birth	Home birth
(a) Fewer options for pain relief, e.g. no epidural	☐	☐
(b) Allows specialists' help, e.g. an obstetrician can perform a C-section if required	☐	☐
(c) Requires parents to make preparations, e.g. buying protective sheets and extra towels	☐	☐
(d) Limits the number of visitors allowed	☐	☐
(e) A familiar environment with all personal belongings nearby	☐	☐

2   Identify the best delivery choice for each of the scenarios below. Write *hospital birth* or *home birth*. **(2 marks)**

(a) Jasmin has a toddler that she continues to breastfeed. She is about to give birth again. She is a healthy 28-year-old woman. A recent scan showed that her baby is in the correct head-down position.

Best option: ....

(b) Mishka is in her forties and struggled to get pregnant. She opted for IVF and now is about to give birth to twins.

Best option: ....

3   Discuss *two* advantages of choosing home birth. **(4 marks)**

....

....

....

....

....

....

....

....

The role of the birth partner see p. 45

1 Read and circle ◯. A birth partner supports the pregnant woman.
   Do the statements refer to the *physical* support (P) or *emotional* support (E)
   that may be offered by a birth partner?   **(5 marks)**

   (a) Encouraging the pregnant woman during labour by telling her she can do it   P / E

   (b) Reassuring her by explaining what is happening   P / E

   (c) Passing her objects that she needs   P / E

   (d) Organising things at home so she can focus on labour   P / E

   (e) Arranging transport to the hospital if needed   P / E

2 Lena and Hussain are married and expecting their first baby. Lena would like
   her husband to be present at the birth but Hussain is not sure how he could help.
   Discuss the emotional and physical support he could offer Lena during her
   pregnancy and labour. The answer has been started for you.   **(8 marks)**

   Hussain can help a lot. He can offer some physical support, for example in her

   late pregnancy Lena won't be able to do much physical work, so Hussain can help

   with buying things needed for the labour and the baby's arrival.

Workbook

Pain relief in labour 1 and 2 see p. 46–47

1   Read and tick (✓). Which statement matches which method of pain relief?
    Some statements apply to more than one method of pain relief.   **(7 marks)**

> **Tip:** You need to put seven ticks – the same as the number of marks for
> this question.

		Epidural	Entonox	Pethidine	TENS
(a)	A side effect of this method of pain relief is that it gives the pregnant woman a dry mouth.				
(b)	Only a specialist doctor can administer this method of pain relief and it has to be given in a hospital.				
(c)	The pregnant woman is in control of how much of this method of pain relief she wants at a given time.				
(d)	If this method of pain relief is given too close to the middle stage of labour, the baby can struggle with breathing.				
(e)	This method of pain relief numbs the woman from the waist down. It is essential if a C-section is needed.				
(f)	This method of pain relief uses electric patches that block the transmission of pain to the brain.				

2   The text explains how Entonox is used as a method of pain relief.
    Complete the sentences using the words in the box.   **(5 marks)**

> anaesthetic   drowsiness   mouthpiece   nitrous oxide   relieve

Entonox is a mixture of gas and air that a pregnant woman in labour can breathe in via a

.... It consists of .... It is harmless to the baby but can

cause the pregnant woman some minor side effects, e.g. .... Although it is

generally considered safe, it doesn't .... all the pain and a woman may still

need an additional .... A good thing about Entonox is that it can be used

during a water birth.

3   Read and circle ◯. Are the statements about using TENS as a method of
    pain relief in labour *true* or *false*?   **(7 marks)**

    (a) TENS can only be administered in a hospital.   True / False

    (b) TENS can't be used in a water birth.   True / False

    (c) TENS doesn't relieve intense pain.   True / False

    (d) TENS has harmful side effects for the baby.   True / False

    (e) TENS can lower the pregnant woman's blood pressure.   True / False

    (f) TENS works almost immediately.   True / False

    (g) TENS shouldn't be used if the pregnant woman has epilepsy.   True / False

4   Becca is 37 weeks pregnant and considering which methods of pain relief to
    use when she gives birth. She has already given birth to a child and wants to
    have a home birth. Choose *two* methods of pain relief and discuss their
    strengths and weaknesses.   **(8 marks)**

    ....

    ....

    ....

    ....

    ....

    ....

    ....

    ....

    ....

    ....

    ....

    ....

    ....

    ....

    ....

    ....

Workbook

Signs that labour has started and stages of labour see p. 48–49

1   Having a show, the first contractions and waters breaking are all signs that labour has started. Read and circle ◯ the correct words to complete the sentences.   **(3 marks)**

(a) First contractions can be very **regular / irregular**.

(b) A show is a sign that the cervix has started to **open / close**.

(c) When a pregnant woman's waters breaks, fluid is released from the **amniotic sac / bladder**.

2   Complete the sentences using the words in the box.   **(4 marks)**

| 10 cm   cervix   contractions   dilation |

Stage 1: Once labour has started, ... become more regular. They stimulate the

.... to widen. This is referred to as .... The first stage is

over when the cervix opening reaches .... in diameter.

3   Identify the *three* things that happen in stage 2 of labour. Put a tick (✓).   **(3 marks)**

(a) The placenta is delivered.   ☐

(b) The pregnant woman has regular contractions and feels the urge to push.   ☐

(c) Having a show   ☐

(d) Crowning of the head   ☐

(e) Birth of the whole body   ☐

(f) Waters breaking   ☐

4   Explain what happens in stage 3 of labour.   **(3 marks)**

....

....

....

....

....

Assisted birth 1 and 2 see p. 50–51

1   Complete the words with the missing letters.   (5 marks)

(a) e _ _ sio _ _ _ y   (b) ve _ _ _ _ se

(c) per _ _ _ _ m   (d) Cae _ _ _ _ an section

(e) br _ _ _ h

2   Read the definitions. Write the missing words.   (6 marks)

(a) A surgical cut made between the vagina and the anus – it is done to create more
     space for the baby to be born

     ....

(b) A metal instrument fitted around a baby's head to help the delivery

     ....

(c) A condition where the placenta is at the bottom of the uterus and blocks the birth canal

     ....

(d) An area of skin between the vagina and the anus where an episiotomy would be done

     ....

(e) An instrumental method of delivery that involves placing a suction cup on baby's head

     ....

(f) When the baby doesn't turn head down and remains with its feet/bottom pointing
     towards the birth canal

     ....

3   Look at the photo. It shows one of the instruments that can be used to assist labour.
    Name the instrument and state *one* reason why it may be necessary to use it.   (2 marks)

Name: ....

Reason for use: ....

....

....

Workbook

4 Complete the sentences using the words in the box. **(6 marks)**

elective	epidural	general	multiple	oxygen	surgical

A C-section is a .... intervention. It must be performed in a hospital.

The pregnant woman will either be given an ...., in which case she will

remain conscious, or she will be given .... anaesthesia, which will make her

unconscious. An .... C-section is one that is planned. A planned C-section may

be advised if the baby is in a breech position or if there are difficulties with a ....

pregnancy. A C-section can also be performed as an emergency procedure, for example if the

baby is lacking .... and needs to be delivered immediately.

5 Explain the difference between a forceps delivery and ventouse delivery. **(2 marks)**

....

....

....

....

6 Ffion's labour has started. An obstetrician has advised that an episiotomy should
be performed.

(a) Explain what is meant by the term 'episiotomy'. **(2 marks)**

....

....

....

(b) Outline *two* reasons why Ffion needs an episiotomy. **(2 marks)**

1 ....

....

2 ....

....

(c) Ffion has the episiotomy but unfortunately, the baby has still not been delivered.
The obstetrician decides that a C-section is needed urgently. What name is given to
an unplanned C-section? **(1 mark)**

....

....

Immediate postnatal checks 1 and 2 see p. 52–53

1 Which of these babies would be classified as having a normal birth weight?
Tick (✓) *two* options. **(2 marks)**

(a) Sigrid 2.31 kg (5.1 lb) ☐

(b) Rohan 4 kg (8.9 lb) ☐

(c) Priti 3.49 kg (7.7 lb) ☐

(d) Aqsa 3.63 kg (8 lb) ☐

2 What is the typical length of a healthy newborn baby? Tick the correct answer (✓). **(1 mark)**

(a) 45–47 cm ☐

(b) 50–53 cm ☐

(c) 55–58 cm ☐

(d) 60–63 cm ☐

3 Identify *one* measurement or check that is not a part of the APGAR examination.
Tick (✓) the correct answer. **(1 mark)**

(a) Breathing ☐   (b) Head circumference ☐

(c) Muscle tone ☐   (d) Heart rate ☐

(e) Skin colour ☐   (f) Reflexes ☐

4 Mary and Bryn's baby girl, Judith, scored 5 on the APGAR scale in the first minute of
life. After five minutes, this had changed to 9. Help Mary and Bryn understand what the
different scoring in an APGAR examination means.

(a) Briefly outline the condition of a baby who scores 5. **(1 mark)**

....

....

(b) Briefly outline the condition of a baby who scores 9. **(1 mark)**

....

....

5 Circle ◯ the correct words to complete the sentences. **(6 marks)**

    (a) Lanugo is the **fine downy hair / waxy protective substance** that covers a newborn's skin.

    (b) 'Stork marks' is the same thing as **salmon patches / strawberry marks**.

    (c) The typical head circumference of a newborn is **32 / 35** centimetres.

    (d) It is recommended that you **do / don't** wash vernix off after birth.

    (e) Babies born weighing below **2.49 kg (5.5 lb) / 2.95 kg (6.5 lb)** are considered to have a low birth weight.

    (f) The length of the baby is measured when the baby is **standing up / lying down**.

6 Outline *two* functions of lanugo. **(2 marks)**

    1 ....

    2 ....

7 Outline *two* functions of vernix. **(2 marks)**

    1 ....

    2 ....

8 Explain what postnatal checks parents can expect to be done on their baby immediately after birth. **(6 marks)**

....

....

....

....

....

....

....

....

....

....

....

....

Additional postnatal examinations 1 and 2 see p. 54–55

1   Complete the table to explain the physical examination of a newborn.   **(4 marks)**

Condition	Body part or organ	What the condition means
Webbing	Fingers/toes	**(a)**
Cataract	**(b)**	A condition that can affect vision and lead to blindness
Hip dysplasia	Hips	**(c)**
Club foot	Feet	**(d)**
Heart murmur	**(e)**	An abnormality in the way blood is distributed to the rest of the body

2   A heel prick test is an optional test offered by the NHS. Answer the following questions.

   (a) When is the heel prick test usually done?   **(1 mark)**

   Day .... of life

   (b) Name *two* conditions that can be detected by a heel prick test.   **(2 marks)**

   1   ....

   2   ....

3   Outline the reasons for the physical examination of the following body parts in
     the first week of a newborn's life.   **(2 marks)**

   (a) Fontanelles: ....

   ....

   ....

   (b) Palms of the hands: ....

   ....

   ....

Postnatal care 1 and 2 see p. 56–57

1   The statements (a–f) refer to SIDS prevention. Read and tick (✓) *Do* or *Don't.*   **(6 marks)**

		Do	Don't
(a)	Allow the baby to sleep in the parents' bed with them.	☐	☐
(b)	Use air freshener.	☐	☐
(c)	Place the baby on their back when putting them to sleep.	☐	☐
(d)	Place a teddy bear in the cot to keep the baby company.	☐	☐
(e)	Keep the house well ventilated and smoke free.	☐	☐
(f)	Put the cot close to the radiator.	☐	☐

2   As part of SIDS prevention, it is recommended that babies are placed in their cots in a 'feet to foot' position. Explain what is meant by 'feet to foot'.   **(2 marks)**

....

....

....

....

3   Outline the role of a health visitor in supporting the mother after giving birth.   **(4 marks)**

....

....

....

....

....

....

....

....

....

....

4 Isla has booked her six-week postnatal check with her GP. Discuss the importance and purpose of this appointment. The answer has been started for you. **(8 marks)**

The postnatal check is vital to monitor the mother's well-being and health.

....

....

....

....

....

....

....

....

....

....

....

....

....

5 Outline *three* ways Isla's partner can support her after labour. **(3 marks)**

1 ....

....

2 ....

....

3 ....

....

6 Identify *one* other person (not a health professional) who could offer their support to Isla. **(1 mark)**

....

Developmental needs 1–4 see p. 58–61

1 Complete the words with the missing letters. **(4 marks)**

   (a) cog _ _ _ _ _ e

   (b) d _ hy _ _ _ _ _ _ _ n

   (c) we _ _ ing

   (d) mal _ _ _ _ _ _ _ _ _ _

2 Match the developmental needs in the box to the corresponding statement.
Write the correct developmental need in the space provided. **(8 marks)**

> exercise   feeding   fresh air   hygiene   shelter/home
> sleep/rest   socialisation   warmth

   (a) If this need is not met, a child could suffer from malnutrition. ....

   (b) Carers should clean the house regularly, especially areas like the bathroom and kitchen.

   ....

   (c) Carers should include the child in family celebrations, so that the child feels a part of the

   extended family. ....

   (d) Carers should use a thermometer to monitor the temperature in the house.

   ....

   (e) It is important for muscle recovery and to consolidate daily learning.

   ....

   (f) It is particularly good for gross motor skills. ....

   (g) It prevents the development of some pulmonary diseases. ....

   (h) Carers can ensure this need is met by installing a stairgate and other safety measures.

   ....

3 Stuart and Amy are the happy parents of a two-month-old baby girl, Lizzie.
They have both developed an emotional attachment with Lizzie.

   (a) What other name is used for the emotional attachment formed between parents and
their children? **(1 mark)**

   ....

(b) Outline *two* ways in which parents can create an emotional attachment with their children. **(2 marks)**

1 ....

....

2 ....

....

(c) Discuss how Stuart and Amy can meet Lizzie's development needs for sleep and rest, and feeding to help her reach her full potential. The answer has been started for you. **(8 marks)**

Sleep and rest is another developmental need that Stuart and Amy have

to provide for Lizzie.

....

....

....

....

....

....

....

....

....

....

....

....

....

....

....

....

....

Childhood illnesses 1–4 see p. 62–65

1 From the list below, tick (✓) the symptoms that are typical for a child who has developed measles.   (3 marks)

(a) Upset stomach   ☐

(b) Red eyes which are sensitive to light   ☐

(c) White spots on the inside of the mouth   ☐

(d) Seizures   ☐

(e) Runny nose, sneezing and coughing   ☐

(f) Swollen neck glands   ☐

2 Three children felt unwell at a local nursery and have now been collected and taken home. Identify *three* possible illnesses based on the symptoms presented by each child.   (3 marks)

(a) Mathis developed a high temperature. He felt sick and drowsy. He was squinting as he was finding it difficult to see. The nursery worker noticed a rash on his skin. She pressed a glass against it but the rash didn't fade.

   Possible illness: ....

(b) Fabienne initially reported having a headache a few days ago and her forehead was hot to touch. She continued to attend nursery. Today her neck has swelled up and she is struggling to swallow anything.

   Possible illness: ....

(c) Adam developed a high temperature and the carer noticed he had some red spots on his body. His mum decided to keep him at home for a couple of days. She informed the nursery that the spots had become very itchy and filled with fluid. Eventually, they transformed into scabs.

   Possible illness: ....

3 How would a parent/carer recognise that a child is suffering from gastroenteritis? Outline *three* signs/symptoms of this condition.   (3 marks)

1 ....

2 ....

3 ....

4 Explain what is meant by the 'incubation period' of an illness or disease. **(2 marks)**

....

....

....

5 Suhayb's son has developed measles. The GP has told him that it is a notifiable disease.

  (a) Briefly explain what 'notifiable disease' means. **(1 mark)**

....

....

  (b) Name *one* condition, other than measles, that is also a notifiable disease. **(1 mark)**

....

....

6 When a child is ill, it is usually advised that they stay at home until they have finished the course of treatment. Outline *two* reasons why ill children should stay at home. **(2 marks)**

1 ....

....

2 ....

....

7 Lily is five years old. Her parents/carers have decided to keep her at home for a few days as she has developed a fever.

  (a) At what point is a child classified as having a fever? Give your answer in °C. **(1 mark)**

....

  (b) Outline *three* different ways Lily's parents/carers could try to reduce her fever. **(3 marks)**

  1 ....

  2 ....

  3 ....

Emergency medical help see p. 66

1   Put the steps for placing a child in the recovery position in the correct order.
    One has been done for you.   **(6 marks)**

    (a) Stay with the child until the ambulance arrives.   ....

    (b) Lie the child on their back. Kneel by the child's side.   ....*1*.........

    (c) Check that the child's mouth is open and that they are breathing.   ....

    (d) With your other hand, grasp the far leg of the child above the knee
         and pull it up so that their knee is bent at a right angle.   ....

    (e) Place the child's arm closest to you at a right angle to the child,
         with their elbow bent to 90° and palm facing up.   ....

    (f) Cross the other arm over the child's body, placing the back of their
         palm by their opposite cheek. Hold it in place with your hand.   ....

    (g) Pull their leg towards you so that the child rolls to one side, facing you,
         with one of their hands under their face.   ....

2   Identify *two* situations when urgent medical attention is needed for a
    young child.   **(2 marks)**

    1 ....

       ....

    2 ....

       ....

3   Outline *two* actions carers should take to help a child who is having a seizure.   **(2 marks)**

    1 ....

       ....

    2 ....

       ....

Meeting the needs of an ill child 1–3 see p. 67–69

1 Read the examples of different ways of meeting an ill child's needs. What type of need would each one meet? Write *physical* need (P), *intellectual* need (I), *emotional* need (E) or *social* need (S). The first one has been done for you. **(6 marks)**

Statements	Need
(a) Arranging online calls with friends or family	S
(b) Letting the child rest with their favourite blanket covering them and a teddy bear by their side	
(c) Regularly opening the windows to let in fresh air	
(d) Giving them their medication as instructed by the GP or pharmacist	
(e) Role playing being on a hospital ward	
(f) Contacting their school and requesting any schoolwork that can be done at home	
(g) Giving them a colouring book and crayons	

2 Read the treatment guidelines below. Identify the illness that each guideline refers to. **(3 marks)**

(a) Blend or mash food if the child is struggling to swallow; they can take liquids through a straw.

Likely illness: ....

(b) Give plain food, e.g. toast or rice, and provide plenty of water as the child is likely to be dehydrated.

Likely illness: ....

(c) Keep the lights dimmed as the child may be sensitive to bright light. Monitor their temperature to check if the symptoms are getting worse.

Likely illness: ....

3 Give *three* examples of games or activities that could meet the intellectual needs of an ill child. Make sure they are different to those in question 1. Briefly explain why each activity would be suitable. **(6 marks)**

Activity 1: ....

Why it would be suitable: ....

....

Activity 2: ....

Why it would be suitable: ....

....

Activity 3: ....

Why it would be suitable: ....

....

4   Mackenzie and Heidi are caring for their ill grandson, Leo. Discuss how carers
    can meet the social and emotional needs of an ill child. The answer has been
    started for you.   **(8 marks)**

Social needs are important as a child is likely to be very lonely at home. ....

....

....

....

....

....

....

....

....

....

....

....

....

....

Hazard prevention 1–3 see p. 70–72

1 Look at the picture. Annotate the picture identifying *four* different hazards in the kitchen. **(4 marks)**

2 Outline *two* ways of preventing burns and scalds in the kitchen. **(2 marks)**

> **Tip:** Use the picture in question 1 to help you.

1 ....

2 ....

3 Identify the type of hazard in the following examples. For each one, write whether it is a *physical* hazard (PH), *biological* hazard (BH), *fire* hazard (FH) or *security* hazard (SH). **(5 marks)**

	Hazard type
(a) Faulty iron which has been left plugged in	
(b) Mould on the bathroom wall	
(c) Flammable liquids under the kitchen sink	
(d) Broken glass panel on a cupboard	
(e) Broken lock on the garden gate	

4 Explain *two* reasons why children are more prone to accidents than adults. **(4 marks)**

Reason 1: ....

....

Reason 2: ....

....

5 Anaya and Priya are opening a new local nursery. Outline *three* measures they should take to make the bathroom/toilet a safe place for children to use. **(3 marks)**

1 ....

2 ....

3 ....

6 Outline *three* ways in which parents/carers can help to ensure the road safety of children. **(3 marks)**

1 ....

....

2 ....

....

3 ....

....

7 Put the Green Cross Code in the correct order. The first one has been done for you. **(5 marks)**

(a) STOP! Stand on the pavement near the kerb. ....

(b) USE YOUR EYES AND EARS! Look all around for traffic and listen. ....

(c) LOOK and LISTEN! When it is safe, walk straight across the road – do not run. ....

(d) ARRIVE ALIVE! Keep looking and listening whilst you cross. ....

(e) THINK! Find the safest place to cross. ....*1*........

(f) WAIT UNTIL IT IS SAFE TO CROSS! If traffic is coming, let it pass. Then look all around again. ....

Safety labels see p. 73

1 Answer the questions.

(a) Explain what the Age Warning symbol means. **(2 marks)**

....

....

....

(b) Give *two* specific examples of items that would have the Age Warning symbol. **(2 marks)**

1 ....

2 ....

2 Children's nightwear needs to meet specific safety requirements due to the risk of fire.

(a) Name a label that informs the buyer that the children's nightwear is safe. **(1 mark)**

....

(b) Explain how this label needs to be displayed on the nightwear. **(2 marks)**

....

....

....

3 Rob and Laura are preparing to open a nursery in their local area. They need to buy some baby equipment. Discuss the importance of checking the safety labels on baby equipment. **(4 marks)**

....

....

....

....

....

....

....

Glossary

Key terms

Accident: An unexpected event that causes injury or damage.

Mia was hurt in an accident yesterday – she fell down the stairs.

Amniotic fluid: A yellow fluid (liquid) formed in the 12 days after conception to surround and protect the embryo and later the foetus.

The embryo is surrounded by amniotic fluid for protection.

Anaesthetic: A pain relief method, often in the form of medication.

An epidural is a popular anaesthetic in labour.

Anomaly: Something which is unusual or different from normal.

The couple went for the anomaly scan at 20 weeks.

Antenatal care: The medical care which is given to a woman during pregnancy.

After confirming her pregnancy, the doctor referred Amara to the antenatal clinic.

Antenatal clinic: Where pregnancy appointments take place.

Assisted birth: When forceps or a ventouse suction cup are used during birth to help with delivery.

The midwife told Diane about what would happen in an assisted birth.

Bacteria: Microorganisms that can cause diseases.

The children were asked to wash their hands to remove any bacteria.

Balanced diet: Eating a variety of foods so your body takes in all the nutrients needed for healthy growth and development.

Saleh eats a balanced diet with lots of fruit and vegetables.

Barrier method of contraception: Barrier methods of contraception provide a physical obstruction that prevents sperm from reaching the egg.

Birth plan: A written record of a pregnant woman's preferred options during labour.

Michael and Samira sat down to work out their preferred birth plan.

Bottle-feed: When a baby is fed with milk from a bottle.

Dads often enjoy bottle-feeding their babies.

Breastfeed: When a mother feeds her baby with milk from her breasts.

Breastfeeding is encouraged in the first few weeks of a baby's life.

Caesarean section: An operation to deliver a baby through a cut in the abdomen.

Sam had to have a caesarean section to deliver her twins.

Cataract: An eye condition where one or both eyes become cloudy.

Dim or blurry vision is one of the first symptoms of a cataract.

Cervix: The lower part of the uterus which leads to the vagina.

Club foot (talipes): When a baby's foot or feet turn inwards.

Hugh was born with talipes.

Cognitive: Related to intellect or thinking skills.

Reading books is an important part of child's cognitive development.

Conception: The point of fertilisation when an embryo starts to form and pregnancy begins.

Contagious: Of a disease that spreads from person to person.

Flu is a contagious illness.

Contraception: Using various methods to prevent pregnancy when having sex.

Contraction: A tightening of the muscles of the uterus.

She was having strong, regular contractions.

Cooperative play: Children play the same game or activity together.

The children discussed their play plans and worked towards the same goal in their cooperative play.

Diagnostic test: A test which is used to discover what is wrong and whether a baby has a specific condition.

The diagnostic test showed that their baby had a high chance of having a health condition.

Disposable nappy: A nappy that is used once and thrown away.

Alicia decided not to use disposable nappies because of their impact on the environment.

Down's syndrome: A lifelong condition which causes a learning disability that can be mild to severe. It affects around 1 in 600 babies.

Embryo: The fertilised egg developing in its mother's womb up to the first eight weeks of pregnancy.

Epidural: A form of pain relief during labour which is given by an anaesthetist.

I wrote in my birth plan that I would like to have an epidural.

Episiotomy: A cut which is made in the area between the vagina and anus to help with childbirth. This is stitched after the birth.

The doctor gave her an episiotomy to help with the delivery of her baby.

Fallopian tube: Either one of the pair of tubes in a woman's body that carry the egg to the uterus.

Feet to foot: A way of putting a baby to bed to help prevent SIDS – the baby's feet should be touching the end of the cot.

Sami always puts his baby to sleep in the 'feet to foot' position.

Fertilisation: When the woman's egg joins with the man's sperm; this process happens in the fallopian tubes.

Artificial fertilisation is an option if a couple can't conceive naturally.

Fertility/fertile: The ability to conceive and produce babies.

Lots of different factors can affect men's and women's fertility.

Foetal alcohol syndrome (FAS): Intellectual and physical problems in a child caused by the mother drinking alcohol during pregnancy.

Jay has speech difficulties because he has foetal alcohol syndrome.

Foetus: An unborn baby more than eight weeks after fertilisation, after the organs have started to develop.

Fontanelles: The soft areas on a baby's head where the skull bones have not yet fused together. One is at the front of the head at the top, and the other towards the back. These soft areas allow the skull some flexibility during childbirth. The skull bones gradually fuse together in the first year or so.

You must be very gentle when you wash a baby's head as the fontanelles are so soft.

Food poisoning: Illness caused by eating bacteria in contaminated food.

Jamie always washes his hands before preparing meals to help to prevent food poisoning.

Forceps: A metal instrument similar to a pair of tongs which are made in the shape of a baby's head to help with delivery.

The doctor used forceps to deliver the baby.

Gestational diabetes: A condition in which a woman has too much glucose (sugar) in her blood during pregnancy. This can cause a range of issues such as jaundice, pre-eclampsia or premature birth.

Kerry and her unborn baby were monitored very closely because she had gestational diabetes.

GP (General Practitioner): A doctor who is based at a local surgery.

Riz went to see her GP to confirm her pregnancy.

Gross motor skills: Use and coordination of the large muscles in the body.

Climbing the tree involved using gross motor skills.

Hazard: Something that may cause you or others harm.

Uncovered ponds are a hazard.

Head circumference: The size of a baby's head (measured around the broadest part of the baby's forehead, above the ears and around the back of the head).

The health visitor measured the circumference of the baby's head.

Heart murmur: Sounds made by blood swishing in or near the heart.

The couple were told that their baby might have a heart murmur.

Hip dysplasia: A condition where the hip joint does not work correctly.

Dysplasia is more common in the left hip.

Hormones: There are various types of hormones; they are chemicals which are produced by the body to help influence how cells and tissues work.

Identical twins: Two children born to the same mother at the same time who developed from the same egg.

Jayden and Robbie are identical twins – nobody can tell them apart.

Immunisation/vaccination: A way of protecting a person from a disease by giving them an injection of a vaccine.

Zofia had not had all her immunisations before she became pregnant.

Implantation: When a fertilised egg burrows into the lining of the uterus.

Implantation day may vary depending on when you ovulated and when you had sex.

Impotence: A medical condition when a man can't have or can't maintain an erection and so can't have sex.

Instrumental delivery: When forceps or a ventouse suction cup are used during birth to help with delivery.

The midwife told Diane about what would happen in an assisted birth.

Intrauterine: Inside the uterus.

An IUD is an example of an intrauterine contraceptive method.

Labour: The process of having a baby from the start of contractions to the delivery of the placenta.

Mel was in labour for 12 hours with her first baby, but this was much shorter second time around.

Lanugo: A type of soft, fine hair covering that develops on the baby's body at around the 22nd week of pregnancy.

Listeriosis: A bacterial infection caused by listeria, a bacterium found in fermented cheese.

A woman may become ill with listeriosis after eating contaminated food.

Menopause: The time when a woman stops having periods.

Geeta is going through the menopause.

Menstrual cycle: The monthly process of ovulation and menstruation in a woman's body.

To try to work out when she was most fertile, Josie and her partner decided to track her menstrual cycle.

Menstruation: Period (the monthly blood flow from a woman's uterus when a woman is not pregnant).

Menstruation usually takes place once a month.

Mercury: A chemical element.

Tuna contains mercury.

Midwife: A nurse who delivers the baby and conducts antenatal appointments.

Miscarriage: The loss of a pregnancy before 24 weeks.

Aliza suffered a miscarriage during her last pregnancy.

Neural tube: Part of the central nervous system, formed in the embryo shortly after conception.

Non-barrier method of contraception: A method of contraception that uses hormones or other substances to prevent pregnancy by stopping the release of an egg.

Imogen didn't like the idea of her partner using a condom, so she opted for a non-barrier method of contraception.

Non-identical twins: Two children born to the same mother at the same time who developed from two different eggs.

Lucy and Tom are non-identical twins, as twins of a different sex cannot be identical.

Notifiable disease: A disease that must be reported to a government authority.

Mumps is a notifiable disease.

Obesity: Being very overweight with too much body fat.

The Government was concerned about rising obesity in the population.

Obstetrician: A doctor specialising in labour who performs C-sections

Oestrogen: A female reproductive hormone.

Ovary: Either one of the pair of organs in a woman's body that produces eggs.

Ovulation: The point in a woman's menstrual cycle when an egg is released.

Pelvic floor exercise: An exercise to strengthen the muscles around the bladder, bottom, vagina or penis.

Anya does her pelvic floor exercises every morning.

Penis: The part of a man's body that is used for urinating and sex.

Placenta: An organ which develops inside the uterus during pregnancy, providing oxygen and nutrients to the foetus through the umbilical cord.

Placenta praevia: When the placenta is low in the uterus and blocks the entrance to the cervix.

Postnatal care: The care given to a new mother and her baby after birth.

Amayah told her sister that she had had excellent postnatal care after the baby was born.

Pre-conception health: The health influences and risk factors of both parents who are planning to conceive, for example type of diet or drinking alcohol.

For her pre-conception health, Gemma was advised to give up smoking before trying to conceive.

Pre-eclampsia: A potentially serious condition which is caused by problems with the placenta leading to a loss of nutrients for the baby.

The blood test revealed that Jenny was at risk of pre-eclampsia.

Progesterone: A female reproductive hormone.

Reproduction: The process of having babies.

The biology teacher announced that today we would be learning about human reproduction.

Reusable nappy: A nappy that is washed and used again.

Dhanya chose to use reusable nappies as she thought they would be more comfortable for her baby.

Risk: The possibility of harm being caused.

Amira cut the children's grapes into quarters to help to prevent the risk of choking.

Risk assessment: A list of potential hazards and the measures in place to help prevent accidents and harm.

The childminder made a risk assessment of the garden.

Salmonella: A type of bacteria.

Charlotte got salmonella poisoning from drinking a smoothie that had a raw egg in it.

Screening test: A test that checks an unborn baby's development and identifies the risk of specific health problems or conditions.

All mothers are offered screening tests during their pregnancy.

Self-esteem: An individual's confidence in their own abilities and worth.

Grace's self-esteem was boosted when she first rode her bike without help.

Seminal vesicle: One of a pair of glands which are situated each side of the bladder in a man's body. During ejaculation, the seminal vesicles add fluid and nutrients to the sperm to produce semen.

Show: A sign that labour has started, when the plug of mucus in the cervix is released.

Pola called her birth partner to say that she'd had a show.

SIDS (sudden infant death syndrome): When an apparently healthy baby dies without a clear medical explanation in the first six months of their life.

Controlling the temperature of the baby's bedroom is one of the ways of preventing SIDS.

Sign: Evidence that something is happening.

Socialisation: Learning social skills, like good manners or family customs.

Children learn socialisation when surrounded by others.

Sperm duct/epididymis: A long tube in a man's body in which the sperm matures and is stored.

Sterilise: The process of killing harmful bacteria, for example on babies' bottles.

Before making up the bottles with babies' milk, it is important to sterilise them.

Stillbirth: A birth when the baby is born dead after a pregnancy of 24 weeks or more.

Symptom: A feeling of illness, or a physical or mental change, that is caused by something.

Desi had all of the symptoms of chickenpox around ten days after his first visit to nursery.

Testis (plural testes)/testicle: The part of a man's body that produces and stores sperm.

Testosterone: A male hormone which helps with sperm production.

Topping and tailing: A way of cleaning a baby using cotton wool and a bowl of warm water.

Topping and tailing is a great way to clean a baby.

Toxoplasmosis: A parasitic disease caused by eating infected food.

You should always wash your fruit and vegetables before eating to prevent toxoplasmosis.

Trimester: Any of the three-month periods that a pregnancy is divided into.

The second trimester is usually the easiest.

Umbilical cord: A long structure, a bit like a tube, that connects an unborn baby to its mother's placenta.

The umbilical cord was clamped and cut after the baby was born and the placenta delivered.

Urethra: The tube that carries urine from the bladder out of the body. In men it also carries sperm.

Uterus/womb: The part of a woman's body in which a baby develops before it is born.

Vaccine: Something injected into a person's body to protect them against a disease.

The girls are having their rubella vaccine at school tomorrow.

Vagina: The passage in a woman's body that connects the outer sex organs to the uterus.

Vas deferens: The tube that sperm pass through on their way out of a man's body.

Ventouse: A type of suction cup, which attaches to a baby's head, used to help to deliver a baby.

Rick told his mum that their baby had needed a ventouse delivery.

Vernix: A white waxy protective substance which covers a baby's skin whilst it is in the uterus.

Waters break: A sign that labour has started, when the amniotic fluid is released from the amniotic sac.

Jessica's waters broke when she was in the supermarket.

Wean/weaning: Start to move babies from milk towards solid food.

Jeanette decided to wean her baby after talking to the health visitor.

Command words

Analyse: Separate or break down information into parts and identify their characteristics or elements. Explain the pros and cons of a topic or argument and make reasoned comments. Explain the impacts of actions using a logical chain of reasoning.

Annotate: Add information, for example, to a table, diagram or graph until it is final. Add all the needed or appropriate parts.

Calculate: Get a numerical answer showing how it has been worked out.

Choose: Select an answer from options given.

Circle: Select an answer from options given.

Compare and contrast: Give an account of the similarities and differences between two or more items or situations.

Complete: Add all the needed or appropriate parts. Add information, for example, to a table, diagram or graph until it is final.

Create: Produce a visual solution to a problem (for example: a mind map, flow chart or visualisation).

Describe: Give an account including all the relevant characteristics, qualities or events. Give a detailed account of.

Discuss: Present, analyse and evaluate relevant points (for example, for/against an argument).

Draw: Produce a picture or diagram.

Evaluate: Make a reasoned qualitative judgement considering different factors and using available knowledge/experience.

Explain: Give reasons for and/or causes of. Use words or phrases such as 'because', 'therefore' or 'this means' in answers.

Fill in: Add all the needed or appropriate parts. Add information, for example, to a table, diagram or graph until it is final.

Identify: Select an answer from options given. Recognise, name or provide factors or features.

Justify: Give good reasons for offering an opinion or reaching a conclusion.

Label: Add information, for example, to a table, diagram or graph until it is final. Add all the necessary or appropriate parts.

Outline: Give a short account, summary or description.

State: Give factors or features. Give short, factual answers.

Answers

The answer pages contain examples of answers that could be given to the questions from the Revision Guide and Workbook. There may be other acceptable answers.

Practise it! activities 20–73

Page 21

1   As a result of smoking, the egg may not be released from the ovary on time. Smoking also leads to changes in the lining of the uterus, preventing the correct implantation of a fertilised egg. **(2)**

2   Any *two* from:
   - being overweight
   - drinking alcohol
   - taking drugs
   - smoking cigarettes **(2)**

Page 22

1   Open spina bifida **(1)**

2   In pregnancy, it is easier to catch a disease and the symptoms can be much worse. If the disease passes to the unborn child, it may lead to serious complications, including stillbirth. Some vaccinations can be given during pregnancy; when this happens, the antibodies pass to the child and give them early protection from the disease. **(3)**

Page 23

1   Barrier methods create a physical obstruction that stops the sperm from reaching the egg. They are used externally, that is, they can be put on the penis or into the vagina, and then be easily taken out. **(2)**

2   Any *one* from: female condom (femidom)/ diaphragm/cap **(1)**

Page 25

1   A contraceptive implant is inserted under the skin of the arm. It works by slowly releasing synthetic progesterone, which prevents ovulation, meaning there is no egg for the sperm to meet. **(2)**

2   An IUS is not easily available as it requires a doctor or a nurse to put it in place. It contains hormones that can cause unpleasant side effects, like mood swings. **(2)**

Page 26

1   Sample answer: A woman could observe the changes in her mucus. When it is clear and slippery, she is at her most fertile. A couple has less chance of getting pregnant if they have sex when the mucus is thicker and creamier later in the cycle. **(2)**

2   Sample answer: The woman needs to have a regular cycle to be able to count her days correctly; the method can easily go wrong if the cycle is out of synch. Additionally, couples are limited to only having sex on certain days of the month, which cannot be changed; some couples may find this an inconvenience. **(4)**

Page 28

1   Releasing mature eggs during ovulation; releasing the sex hormones, i.e. oestrogen and progesterone **(2)**

2   The most fertile day is when ovulation happens; however, as sperm live longer than the egg, fertile days are counted as being for seven days prior to ovulation, ovulation day, and two days after; i.e. days 8–16 of a typical 28-day menstrual cycle. **(3)**

Page 29

1   To produce sperm; to release testosterone **(2)**

2 Diagram to show the journey of the sperm as follows: testes → epididymis/sperm duct → vas deferens → seminal vesicles → urethra. **(5)**

Page 31

1 When a fertilised egg burrows into the lining of the uterus **(1)**

2 A fertilised egg divides itself while travelling down the fallopian tube. As it reaches the uterus, it will burrow itself into the womb lining. **(2)**

Page 32

1 Both 'embryo' and 'foetus' refer to the unborn baby, but 'embryo' is used when talking about early pregnancy (up to the 8th week) whilst 'foetus' refers to the baby after the eighth week. **(2)**

2 It produces the hormones that are needed to maintain the pregnancy; it supplies the nutrients that will be taken to the baby via the umbilical cord. **(2)**

Page 33

1 Identical twins are created from one egg fertilised by one sperm that splits into two before implantation. **(2)**

2 Sample answer: There are two placentas, one for each twin. **(1)**

Page 34

1 Her breasts are likely to feel heavier/swollen; her nipples will become darker. **(2)**

2 Sample answer: missed period; feelings of tiredness and fatigue **(2)**

Page 35

1 Sample answer: A GP advises the pregnant woman about how any pre-existing medical conditions she has may affect the pregnancy; refers her to a specialist if necessary. **(2)**

2 An obstetrician would be called if there were any complications during the pregnancy, e.g.

if the baby was likely to suffer from open spina bifida. They could advise on difficult cases, prescribe specific medications or treatment, and perform a C-section if needed. **(3)**

Page 37

1 Sample answer: examination of the uterus; listening to the baby's heartbeat **(2)**

2 It is important to regularly check the pregnant woman's weight gain to make sure the baby is growing as expected and to identify potential problems, like gestational diabetes or pre-eclampsia if the woman is gaining too much weight. If a pregnant woman loses weight, this can be a sign that the baby isn't growing or has died. **(2)**

Page 39

1 Progress in the growth of the foetus and whether pregnancy is single or multiple **(2)**

2 Any *one* from:
- amniocentesis
- CVS **(1)**

Page 42

1 Sample answer: pâté **(1)**

2 Sample answer: Colostrum helps to build up the baby's immune system, which will protect them from various infections and diseases; it is a great bonding opportunity for mother and baby and it helps them to form an emotional attachment. **(2)**

Page 44

1 Sample answer: access to specialist staff and equipment; greater choice of pain relief options, e.g. an epidural **(2)**

2 Sample answer: A hospital birth may be recommended to women who have not given birth before, especially if there are known complications, such as the baby is in a breech position, in which case a C-section might be needed. **(2)**

Page 45

1 Any *two* from:
- baby's father
- other family member (e.g. grandmother, sister)
- a friend **(2)**

2 Sample answer: The pregnant woman will feel less anxious as her partner will support her emotionally. **(1)**

Page 47

1 Sample answer: The pregnant woman is in control of the dosage; it can be used during a water birth. **(2)**

2 Sample answer: It can affect the baby if it is given too close to delivery. **(2)**

Page 49

1 Any *one* from:
- Having a show (the mucus plug comes out of the vagina)
- Contractions (the uterus is preparing to push)
- Waters breaking (the amniotic fluid is released from the amniotic sac) **(2)**

2 In stage 3, the placenta detaches from the uterus. Contractions continue in order to push the placenta through the vagina. **(2)**

Page 51

1 Any *one* from:
- forceps
- ventouse **(1)**

2 Sample answer: The baby is in a breech position; the baby is not getting enough oxygen. **(2)**

Page 53

1 Appearance, pulse, grimace, activity, respiration **(5)**

2 Sample answer: salmon patches; strawberry marks **(2)**

Page 55

1 The health professional flashes a special torch into the baby's eyes; they are looking to see if there is a red reflection in the irises. **(2)**

2 If the red reflection is not there, there is a possibility that the baby has an eye condition that requires medical treatment. A common one is a cataract. **(2)**

Page 57

1 Sample answer: Always place the baby on their back when putting them in their cot; don't smoke in the house. **(2)**

2 Others can support the new mother in many ways, including physical and emotional support. For example, the partner could be responsible for night feeding which would give the mother time to relax and sleep. Friends could help by doing the grocery shopping or cooking and delivering meals. A new mother is likely to be occupied with her baby and may not have time to do her own shopping or cooking. Finally, the family can help with organising transport if the mother needs to go to a doctor's appointment as she is unlikely to be able to drive herself straight after giving birth. **(4)**

Page 61

1 Sample answer: shelter/home; fresh air; opportunities for listening and talking; routine **(4)**

2 Stimulation is important because as a child uses their senses to experience the world, they create new brain pathways – this means that they are learning. **(2)**

Page 65

1 It means that the disease can spread very quickly and people can catch it easily by being near someone who is ill. **(2)**

2 Sample answer: sudden, watery diarrhoea; vomiting **(2)**

Page 66

1 Sample answer: The child has stopped breathing; the child is having a seizure. **(2)**

2 Clear the area around them and remove any objects the child could hurt themselves on; place soft objects around them to prevent injury; once the seizure has stopped, place the child in the recovery position. **(3)**

Page 69

1 Sample answer: practising language skills by talking and listening to them; contacting their school for schoolwork that can be completed at home **(2)**

2 Emotional needs are important because the way a child feels emotionally will affect their recovery – a happy child is more likely to recover than a stressed/anxious one. This is due to different hormones being released when someone is happy or stressed. **(2)**

Page 72

1 Sample answer: animal faeces; garden equipment that has been left out (e.g. mower) **(2)**

2 Sample answer: Remove any animal faeces straight away; keep garden equipment stored safely in a locked shed. **(2)**

Page 73

1 Sample answer: baby car seat; feeding bottle sanitiser **(2)**

2 Sample answer: CE or UKCA label **(1)**

Workbook answers 74–114

Page 74

1 The health of both would-be parents' *before* conception, including factors such as age, weight, smoking, alcohol and drugs **(2)**

2 **(a)** Zain plays an important role as his sperm will fertilise the egg; low-quality sperm (or a low sperm count) will prevent successful conception. **(2)**

  (b) 1 Stop smoking; 2 Reduce the amount of alcohol he drinks or cut it out completely.

  Note that ambiguous statements, e.g. 'go on diet', 'be healthy', are not sufficient. **(2)**

3 **(a)** Women **(b)** Men

  (c) Women and men **(3)**

4 For women, fertility declines after the age of 35. Women also have a significant risk of giving birth to a child with Down's syndrome after the age of 40. Once they go through the menopause, they won't be able to get pregnant. Men can father a child until they reach a late age but the quality of their sperm decreases as they get older, meaning more attempts may be needed to successfully fertilise an egg. Hence, the best age to consider having a baby (from a health standpoint only) is between 20 and 30. **(4)**

Page 75

1 Any *two* from:
  - Broccoli
  - Chickpeas
  - Brussels sprouts
  - Citrus fruits **(2)**

2 **(a)** True **(c)** True

  (b) False **(d)** True **(4)**

3 Gurveen, your immune system will be weaker in pregnancy, so you are more likely to catch common flu or a similar disease. Flu can pass through the placenta to the unborn baby and cause serious complications. Being vaccinated decreases your chances of catching flu. **(3)**

4 **(a)** Whooping cough

  (b) Rubella

  (c) Flu **(3)**

Page 76

1 It is a barrier method. A man puts a condom on his erect penis before it enters the vagina. This means that his sperm will be caught inside the condom and won't reach the egg. **(3)**

2 92–96% diaphragm/cap; 98% male condom; 95% female condom **(3)**

3 Any *one* from:
   - Can be put in discreetly several hours before sexual intercourse
   - No serious side effects
   - No need to take any hormones **(1)**

4 Any *two* from:
   - They can interrupt sexual pleasure.
   - They can slip off, split or tear.
   - They are single use so you need a new one each time. **(2)**

5 **(a)** and **(b)** **(2)**

Page 77

1 It thickens the mucus at the entrance to the vagina so that the sperm cannot reach the egg, hence fertilisation won't occur. **(2)**

2 **(a)** contraceptive implant – (vii)

   (b) combined pill – (v)

   (c) IUD – (vi)

   (d) contraceptive injection – (iii)

   (e) POP – (i)

   (f) IUS – (ii)

   (g) emergency contraceptive pill – (iv) **(7)**

3 **(a)** An IUS is the most suitable method. A contraceptive implant or injection would also be suitable.

   (b) Contraceptive implant or POP

   (c) The emergency contraceptive pill is most suitable. (An IUD is possible but it is not the best solution in this scenario.)

   (d) Combined pill or an IUS **(4)**

4 IUDs and IUSs are two popular methods of contraception. The side effects of using the IUS are similar to those of using the POP. IUSs contain progesterone, which can lead to mood swings and acne. On the positive side, it makes periods lighter, which is good if a woman is already suffering from heavy periods. IUDs don't contain hormones, so may be more appealing to some women who do not tolerate hormonal therapy well. It does make periods heavier and more painful though. So, if a woman is already suffering from heavy periods, an IUD wouldn't be recommended. Both methods last for years, which is good for couples who do not want any daily hassle. They are also highly effective – up to 99% – which is more than condoms. The downside of each is that a woman needs to book an appointment to have them fitted. This procedure can be uncomfortable and there is a risk of infection after having an IUD or IUS fitted. **(6)**

Page 79

1 1 Cervical mucus observation

   2 Temperature method

   3 Calendar method **(3)**

2 **(a)** periods

   (b) ovulation; avoids

   (c) 99% **(3)**

3 **(a)** True   **(b)** False

   (c) False   **(d)** True

   (e) True **(5)**

4 **(a)** Sharan could measure her body temperature daily in the morning. She should be looking for a pattern of a slightly increased temperature midway through her cycle. After three days of a steady temperature increase, the remaining days are less fertile until a new cycle begins.

   (b) Sharan could use the calendar method and count the days in her cycle. Assuming her cycle is 28 days long, she would know that ovulation happens on the 14th day, which is when she is the most likely to get pregnant. She would avoid having unprotected sex seven days prior to that and two days after.

Sharan could also observe her mucus. When her fertile days are approaching, her mucus will become clear and slippery. If she wants to avoid getting pregnant, she should wait until the mucus is thicker or totally dry before having sex. **(6)**

Page 80

1 **(a)** Vagina   **(b)** Oestrogen

  (c) Uterus   **(d)** Fallopian tube

  (e) Cervix **(5)**

2 **(a)** Uterus/womb   **(b)** Cervix

  (c) Ovary **(3)**

3 **(a)** Fallopian tube(s)   **(b)** Cervix

  (c) Vagina   **(d)** Womb/uterus **(4)**

4 There is one ovary on each side of the uterus. They store the eggs until they are mature and ready to be released. They release one egg each month. They release the sex hormones, oestrogen and progesterone. **(2)**

Page 81

1 **(a)** Menstruation

  (b) Ovulation

    Fertility is low

    Fertility is very high

    Fertility is low **(5)**

2 **(a)** 4   **(b)** 1   **(c)** 3

  (d) 2   **(e)** 5 **(4)**

3 **(a)** True   **(b)** False

  (c) False   **(d)** False **(4)**

Page 82

1 **(a)** Epididymis

(b) Vas deferens

(c) Urethra

(d) Seminal vesicles **(4)**

2 **(a)** Vas deferens   **(b)** Penis

  (c) Urethra **(3)**

3 **(a)** Testes   **(b)** Penis

  (c) Seminal vesicles   **(d)** Epididymis **(4)**

4 A narrow tube running through the length of the penis that transports sperm and urine out of the man's body. **(2)**

Page 83

1 Word 1: ovulation

  Word 2: fallopian tube(s)

  Word 3: uterus/ womb

  Word 4: implantation

  Word 5: embryo **(5)**

2 Boy/male **(1)**

3 **(a)** False   **(b)** True

  (c) True   **(d)** False **(4)**

4 Fertilisation – inside either of the fallopian tubes; implantation – inside the uterus, on either side of the uterus wall. **(2)**

Page 84

1 **(a)** Liquid; sac   **(b)** Tube

  (c) Organ; uterus **(5)**

2 **(a)** (iii), (iv)   **(b)** (i), (v)

  (c) (ii), (vi) **(6)**

3 After week 8 **(1)**

4 **(a)** Oxygen; water; food nutrients; alcohol

  (b) Carbon dioxide; urea

  (c) Blood **(7)**

Page 85

1. **(a)** Non-identical **(b)** Identical
   (c) Non-identical **(d)** Identical
   (e) Identical **(5)**

2. **(a)** Premature **(b)** More likely
   (c) Increase **(d)** Higher **(4)**

3. **(a)** This happens when more than one egg is released during ovulation and each egg is fertilised with a different male sperm. **(2)**

   (b) There will be two separate placentas, one for each twin. **(1)**

Page 86

1. 1 Tiredness/fatigue

   2 Nausea

   3 Late/missed period **(3)**

2. Breasts are likely to become larger and feel sore; the nipples may darken and stand out more. **(2)**

3. **(a)** True **(b)** False
   (c) True **(d)** False **(4)**

4. **(b)** Early pregnancy symptoms are caused by the surge in the hormones progesterone and hCG.

   (d) Frequent urination can also affect women in late pregnancy when the growing baby puts pressure on the bladder. **(2)**

Page 87

1. The medical support a woman receives during pregnancy **(1)**

2. Any *two* from:
   - screening tests
   - diagnostic tests
   - The pregnant woman's health and that of the unborn baby are monitored by a midwife.
   - antenatal (parenting) classes **(2)**

3. **(a)** (iii) GP **(b)** (i) Midwife

(c) (ii) Obstetrician **(3)**

4. **(a)** OBS **(b)** GP
   (c) MW **(d)** MW **(4)**

5. A midwife monitors the health of a pregnant woman and her baby throughout the pregnancy. They keep a medical record of every visit and arrange all the clinical examinations, including screening tests. They can also lead parenting classes to teach new parents/carers how to care for a baby and what to expect in labour. A midwife delivers babies in normal healthy pregnancies and doesn't perform C-sections. **(3)**

Page 88

1. To calculate the baby's due date **(1)**

2. Any *two* from:
   - To check Oksana's blood group in case she needs a blood transfusion during labour
   - To check her iron levels to make sure she hasn't developed anaemia
   - To check her rhesus factor in case there are harmful antibodies that conflict with baby's blood group. **(4)**

3. **(a)** 110–160 bpm **(b)** High
   (c) Low **(d)** Gain **(4)**

4. **(a)** Blood sample; urine test
   (b) Uterus exam
   (c) Blood sample
   (d) Blood sample; urine test; blood pressure
   (e) Blood sample **(8)**

Page 89

1. **(a)** Screening **(b)** Screening
   (c) Diagnostic **(d)** Screening
   (e) Diagnostic **(5)**

2. **(a)** Anomaly scan **(b)** NIPT
   (c) Amniocentesis **(d)** Dating scan
   (e) NFT **(5)**

3 **CVS** is usually done between week **11** and week **14** of pregnancy, whilst **amniocentesis** is offered later, i.e. between week **15** and week **20**. They both help to diagnose serious conditions, such as **Down's syndrome/ cystic fibrosis** and **cystic fibrosis/Down's syndrome**. The main difference is that in CVS a sample is obtained through the **vagina** whilst in amniocentesis a **needle** is inserted into the uterus. It is monitored by an ultrasound device. **(8)**

4 **(a)** A serious neural tube birth defect caused when the spine and spinal cord do not form correctly in early pregnancy **(2)**

   (b) Amniocentesis **(1)**

5 Any *two* from:
   • Down's syndrome
   • Cleft palate
   • Cystic fibrosis
   • Edwards' syndrome
   • Patau's syndrome
   • Anencephaly
   • Serious cardiac problems. **(2)**

6 **(a)** CVS – chorionic villus sampling

   (b) NFT scan – nuchal fold translucency (scan)

   (c) NIPT – non-invasive prenatal testing **(3)**

Page 91

1 Maciej could learn how to support Magda during labour, for example by measuring her contractions or offering a massage; he could also learn about how to care for the baby after they are born and that could give Magda some time to look after herself. **(4)**

2 **(a)** Raw shellfish, too much tuna, too much oily fish – high levels of mercury in fish and bacteria in raw shellfish can affect the baby's development and could lead to miscarriage.

   (c) Wine and beer – can lead to foetal alcohol syndrome (FAS) which affects the child's intellectual development and internal organs. **(4)**

3 Any *two* from:
   • She should do pelvic floor exercises to strengthen her pelvic muscles.
   • She should quit smoking and avoid passive smoking.
   • She shouldn't go horse riding or skiing.
   • She should avoid being stressed.
   • She should avoid pollution.
   • She should get enough sleep. **(2)**

4 **(a)** Salmonella – (iv)

   (b) Colostrum – (ii)

   (c) Topping and tailing – (iii)

   (d) Toxoplasmosis – (vi)

   (e) Mastitis – (v)

   (f) Listeria – (i) **(7)**

5 **(a)** Any *one* from:
   • The baby gets colostrum, which is a substance full of antibodies that will help them stay healthy.
   • It reduces the risk of the baby having an upset stomach.
   • It reduces the risk of SIDS. **(1)**

   (b) Any *one* from:
   • It stimulates the uterus to go back to its original size.
   • It decreases the mother's risk for some cancers. **(1)**

   (c) Any *two* from:
   • Sore/cracked nipples
   • Blocked milk ducts
   • Not enough milk
   • Too much milk
   • Baby has a tongue tie
   • Baby doesn't attach to the breast properly
   • Breast infection **(2)**

Page 93

1 **(a)** Home   **(b)** Hospital

   (c) Home   **(d)** Hospital

(e) Home **(5)**

2 **(a)** Home birth   **(b)** Hospital birth **(2)**

3 One advantage is that the mother is in a familiar environment and that is likely to make her feel more relaxed. She doesn't have to worry about things like travelling to the hospital. Another advantage is that she is not limited to a set number of visitors. The mother can be supported by others, and if she has other children already, they won't have to miss her. This can be particularly important if she is also breastfeeding other children as there won't be any breaks in the feeding routine.

Other advantages include: she won't be separated from her partner after the birth; a familiar midwife will assist the delivery; more privacy. **(4)**

Page 94

1 **(a)** E   **(b)** E   **(c)** P
(d) P   **(e)** P **(5)**

2 Hussain can help a lot. He can offer some physical support, for example in her late pregnancy Lena won't be able to do much physical work, so Hussain can help with buying things needed for the labour and the baby's arrival. If they decide to have a home birth, he can help with the house preparation. If they decide to go to the hospital, he can arrange the transport. He can also support Lena emotionally, for example he can encourage her to push when needed or to relax and ease her anxiety levels. He could also help by voicing Lena's wishes to the hospital staff, so she feels her questions are answered. That will reassure her. Finally, he can show her love and support by holding her hand. Without the birth partner's support, the woman is likely to be more stressed, which can make her labour experience more painful. **(8)**

Page 95

1 **(a)** Entonox

(b) Epidural

(c) Entonox and TENS

(d) Pethidine

(e) Epidural

(f) TENS **(7)**

2 Entonox is a mixture of gas and air that a pregnant woman in labour can breathe in via a **mouthpiece**. It consists of **nitrous oxide**. It is harmless to the baby but can cause the pregnant woman some minor side effects, e.g. **drowsiness**. Although it is generally considered safe, it doesn't **relieve** all the pain and a woman may still need an additional **anaesthetic**. A good thing about Entonox is that it can be used during a water birth. **(5)**

3 **(a)** False   **(b)** True

(c) True   **(d)** False

(e) False   **(f)** True

(g) True **(7)**

4 Two possible pain relief methods are an epidural and Entonox. An epidural is an injection to the spine area that numbs the woman from the waist down, giving almost full pain relief. It is safe for the baby although it can cause problems with the mother's blood pressure. Unfortunately, it can only be given by a specialist doctor in a hospital, so if Becca wants to give birth at home, she won't be able to have an epidural. An alternative is Entonox. This is a mixture of gas and air that a woman inhales, regulating her own intake. This is something Becca could use, as an Entonox canister can be brought home by the midwife. Entonox is also safe for the baby. It can cause minor side effects for the mother, for example it can give her a dry mouth and make her feel lightheaded and drowsy. This may cause her to have problems with focusing on the labour. It also doesn't relieve all the pain, so Becca will still be able to feel the contractions. This can be good as it gives her control over the labour but it also means she will feel some pain. **(8)**

Page 97

1 **(a)** Irregular   **(b)** Open

(c) Amniotic sac **(3)**

2 Stage 1: Once labour has started, **contractions** become more regular. They stimulate the **cervix** to widen. This is referred to as **dilation**. The first stage is over when the cervix opening reaches **10 cm** in diameter. **(4)**

3 **(b), (d), (e)** **(3)**

4 Stage 3 is called the 'afterbirth' because the placenta detaches from the wall of the uterus and is expelled through the vagina. Often, an injection is given to aid the placenta delivery and to reduce any bleeding that the mother may experience. If a woman has had an episiotomy, stitches would be applied in stage 3. **(3)**

Page 98

1 **(a)** Episiotomy

(b) Ventouse

(c) Perineum

(d) Caesarean section

(e) Breech **(5)**

2 **(a)** Episiotomy

(b) Forceps

(c) Placenta praevia

(d) Perineum

(e) Ventouse

(f) Breech position **(6)**

3 **Name:** forceps

Reason for use: If the baby's head gets stuck in the birth canal **(2)**

4 A C-section is a **surgical** intervention. It must be performed in a hospital. The pregnant woman will either be given an **epidural**, in which case she will remain conscious, or she will be given **general** anaesthesia, which will make her unconscious. An **elective** C-section is one that is planned. A planned C-section may be advised if the baby is in a breech position or if there are difficulties with a **multiple** pregnancy. A C-section can also be

performed as an emergency procedure, for example if the baby is lacking **oxygen** and needs to be delivered immediately. **(6)**

5 They are used in similar cases but forceps are a metal tool, similar to a pair of tongs, that are fitted around a baby's head, whilst ventouse is a suction cup that is placed on top of the baby's head when the head is crowning. **(2)**

6 **(a)** An episiotomy is a small cut made between the vagina and the anus to allow more space for the baby to pass through. **(2)**

(b) When forceps are going to be used and the doctor needs better access to the birth canal; when there is a risk of natural tearing during labour, it's better to make a clear surgical cut to minimise the damage **(2)**

(c) Emergency C-section **(1)**

Page 100

1 **(c); (d)** **(2)**

2 **(b)** **(1)**

3 **(b)** **(1)**

4 **(a)** Five is a low score that suggests that the baby needs to be observed and may require minor medical intervention. **(1)**

(b) Nine is a very high score that means that the baby is healthy and doesn't require any specific medical help. **(1)**

5 **(a)** Fine downy hair

(b) Salmon patches

(c) 35

(d) Don't

(e) 2.49 kg (5.5 lb)

(f) Lying down **(6)**

6 **1** Maintaining baby's temperature

2 Binding vernix to the skin **(2)**

7 Any *two* from:

- Protection from bacteria

- Maintaining skin's natural moisture
- Helping the baby move through the birth canal **(2)**

8   In the first minute of a baby's life, parents can expect the midwife or paediatrician to perform an APGAR examination, where five vital signs are checked, namely: breathing, heartbeat, reflexes, muscle tone and skin appearance. If all five are satisfactory, the baby will score 7–10 points, which means they are healthy. The APGAR check is repeated five minutes later. Other than that, the midwife/doctor will take the baby's measurements. They will check the weight and the length. Finally, the head circumference will be checked so that they can monitor the baby's brain development in the future. **(6)**

Page 102

1   **(a)** When fingers/toes are joined together

  (b) Eyes

  (c) Dislocation of the hips/problems with the hip joints

  (d) Feet facing inwards

  (e) Heart **(4)**

2   **(a)** 5 **(1)**

  (b) Any *two* from:
- Cystic fibrosis
- Congenital hypothyroidism
- Sickle cell disease **(2)**

3   **(a)** **Fontanelles:** To see if the skull is not bulging/sunken

  (b) **Palms of the hands:** To see if there are two creases (as one crease may be a sign of Down's syndrome) **(2)**

Page 103

1   **Dos:** place the baby on their back; keep the house well ventilated and smoke free.

  Don'ts: allow the baby to sleep in the parents' bed with them; use air freshener; place a teddy bear in the cot; put the cot close to the radiator. **(6)**

2   'Feet to foot' means that the baby's feet are placed at the bottom of the cot rather than in the middle of the cot. That way, the baby is less likely to slip down under the duvet and possibly suffocate. **(2)**

3   Health visitors see the baby regularly to monitor their growth and record it in the red book. They also keep track of the baby's vaccination programme and discuss it with the parents. Furthermore, they assess the condition of the mother post labour and answer any of her questions. Finally, they can offer advice/information on different aspects of baby care, e.g. how to breastfeed. **(4)**

4   The postnatal check is vital to monitor the mother's well-being and health. During her six-week postnatal appointment, Isla's GP will check the healing of her stitches. This is very important as she may have developed an infection or the stitches could have split open. The GP will look at other aspects of Isla's health too, for example they will check her blood pressure. They will ask Isla about her periods – by week 6 they should have returned to normal, and if not, the GP may need to examine Isla further. They will ask her if there is any unusual discharge from her vagina, which can suggest an infection. Fertility returns within the first month of giving birth, so the GP will advise her on the contraceptive methods she could use. Finally, it is possible that Isla has missed her smear test whilst being pregnant, and this can now be booked for her. **(8)**

5   **1** Do the night feeding.

  2 Drive her to any appointments.

  3 Do the housework. **(3)**

6   Any *one* from:
- Friends
- Grandparents
- Aunts/uncles **(1)**

Page 105

1 (a) Cognitive   (b) Dehydration
   (c) Weaning   (d) Malnutrition (4)

2 (a) Feeding   (b) Hygiene
   (c) Socialisation   (d) Warmth
   (e) Sleep/rest   (f) Exercise
   (g) Fresh air   (h) Shelter/home (8)

3 (a) Bonding/love (1)

   (b) Any *two* from:
       • Skin-to-skin contact, for example by cuddling the baby
       • Talking/singing to the baby
       • Feeding
       • Bathing
       • Giving eye contact
       • Responding to their cries (2)

   (c) Sleep and rest is another developmental need that Stuart and Amy have to provide for Lizzie. Sleep is very important because during a night's sleep the growth hormone is released, meaning that most growing happens at night. As Lizzie is only two months old, she could potentially sleep for up to 16 hours per day. Once she is older and becomes more active, rest will be necessary for muscle recovery after she plays outdoors. Lizzie's parents could ensure a good sleep/rest routine by creating the right sleep environment, e.g. keeping the room temperature at 16–20 °C and making sure there is no blue light shining from the TV. Another important developmental need for Lizzie is feeding. Parents need to provide good quality food that is full of nutrients in the right quantities. As Lizzie is young, she will be fed with milk before moving to more solid foods in few months' time. Having the correct diet is important as otherwise Lizzie may suffer from health problems, like malnutrition if she doesn't get enough nutrients, or obesity if her parents overfeed her. Stuart and Amy must also ensure Lizzie gets enough water to drink. (8)

Page 107

1 (b); (c); (e) (3)

2 (a) **Possible illness:** meningitis
   (b) **Possible illness:** mumps
   (c) **Possible illness:** chickenpox (3)

3 Any *three* from:
   • Sudden watery diarrhoea
   • Upset stomach
   • Vomiting
   • Mild fever
   • Aches and pains (3)

4 'Incubation period' means the days between when a child catches an illness and when they develop the symptoms of it. (2)

5 (a) 'Notifiable disease' means that you have to inform the child's GP as it poses a danger to the wider public if it spreads further. (1)

   (b) Either *one* of:
       • Meningitis   • Mumps (1)

6 1 It gives the body time to naturally fight the illness whilst resting.
   2 It prevents the spread of contagious diseases. (2)

7 (a) 38 °C (1)
   (b) 1 Give her plenty of fluids to drink.
       2 Dress her in loose clothes.
       3 Run her a cool bath. (3)

Page 109

1 Correct order – 1: b; 2: e; 3: f; 4: d; 5: g; 6: c; 7: a (6)

2 Any *two* from:
   • The child is choking.
   • The child is having a seizure.
   • The child is unresponsive.
   • The child is having breathing difficulties.
   • The child is turning blue.
   • The child has a high fever. (2)

3 Any *two* from:
- Clear the area around the child of objects that could cause them harm.
- Place blankets or cushions around the child.
- Once the seizure has stopped, place the child in the recovery position. **(2)**

Page 110

1 **(a)** Social   **(b)** Emotional

   (c) Physical   **(d)** Physical

   (e) Social   **(f)** Intellectual

   (g) Intellectual **(6)**

2 **(a)** Mumps or tonsillitis

   (b) Gastroenteritis

   (c) Meningitis or mumps **(3)**

3 **Activity 1:** reading a book

   Why it would be suitable: a child will be exposed to written language and can improve literacy.

   Activity 2: watch educational programmes

   Why it would be suitable: it doesn't require much action from the child letting them relax; it has educational value as it aids their understanding of the world.

   Activity 3: bingo

   Why it would be suitable: gives contact with numbers, hence good for maths skills (numeracy).

   Other answers are also possible. **(6)**

4 Social needs are important as a child is likely to be very lonely at home. They may be concerned that they are losing touch with their friends and family. Mackenzie and Heidi should use a laptop or a smartphone to FaceTime Leo's other relatives or friends. Leo may also be missing out on basic social interactions, like going shopping with his mum, so role playing shop assistant could be a good option to compensate for that. That way Leo can still learn manners, like saying 'please' and 'thank you'. Emotional needs are also important. Leo may be upset by staying at home and this can make his recovery slower due to stress hormones being released. His grandparents should try to keep him in a good mood. This could be achieved by skin-to-skin contact, like giving him cuddles or stroking his head when he is upset. Leo probably has his favourite objects, maybe a teddy bear or favourite pyjamas that he could wear. Those would make him happy. Finally, it is important that Leo knows he is ill and getting better, so his grandparents should explain to him the nature of his illness and treatment in a way Leo can understand and so that he doesn't feel guilty about being ill. **(8)**

Page 112

1 Answers may include: Sharp knives left on the counter; hot pan on the hob; spilt liquid; kettle cord; blind cord hanging loose; chemicals stored in an easily accessible place. **(4)**

2 Any *two* from:
- Always supervise a child in the kitchen.
- Install a cooker guard.
- Turn pan handles inwards towards the wall.
- Use a cordless kettle or keep the flex well out of reach.
- Keep a fire blanket or fire extinguisher nearby. **(2)**

3 **(a)** FH   **(b)** BH   **(c)** FH   **(d)** PH

   (e) SH **(5)**

4 **Reason 1:** children are small/short so they may not see all hazards and also may not be seen by others.

   Reason 2: young children haven't developed their muscle coordination yet – they may walk unsteadily and trip easily, especially when walking up/down the stairs. **(4)**

5 Any *three* from:
- Keep chemicals, like bleach, locked away.
- Clean the toilet regularly.
- Lower the temperature of the water boiler.

- Clear up any spillages straight away.
- Teach personal hygiene. **(3)**

6 Any *three* from:
- Use reins when walking with young children.
- Let the child walk on the inside of the pavement.
- Dress them in high-visibility clothes.
- Use child locks in a car.
- Play away from traffic.
- Make sure the car is fitted with an age-appropriate car seat.
- Teach children the Green Cross Code. **(3)**

7 Correct order – 1: e; 2: a; 3: b; 4: f; 5: c; 6: d **(5)**

Page 114

1 (a) It means that an item you buy is not recommended for small children below three years of age. This is most likely because the item may have small parts that could be swallowed and lead to suffocation/choking. **(2)**

(b) 1 LEGO® bricks

2 Board games **(2)**

2 (a) Low flammability (meets BS 5722 standards) **(1)**

(b) It needs to be permanently and securely attached and resistant to washing, e.g. imprinted on the inner label of the garment. **(2)**

3 Different items can pose different safety risks, so it is important to know which label should be on which object. A bottle steriliser is likely to have a Kitemark as it is electrical equipment. The Kitemark means that the product meets BSI standards. Some non-electric items, like feeding bottles, could have a CE mark, which means that they can be sold in the EU. Recently, the UK introduced its own version of this European mark, called UKAS. The Lion Mark states that an item is safe as well as being educational and suitable for children's play. This label can only be found on toys. Finally, nightwear needs to be fire resistant, so labels need to show they comply with the regulations. **(4)**

Acknowledgements

The authors and publishers acknowledge the following sources of copyright material and are grateful for the permissions granted. While every effort has been made, it has not always been possible to identify the sources of all the material used, or to trace all copyright holders. If any omissions are brought to our notice, we will be happy to include the appropriate acknowledgements on reprinting.

Thanks to the following for permission to reproduce images:

Cover: Peter Dazeley/GI; Inside: Alonzo Design/GI; Moorsky/GI; Alonzo Design/GI; Moorsky/GI; Dorling Kindersley/GI(X3); Alila Medical Media/Shutterstock(X3); Lauren Shavell/GI; Stocktrek Images/GI; Ted Horowitz/GI; Green Cross Code © 2015 North Yorkshire County Council; BSI Kitemark logo is used with permission from the British Standards Institution; Lion Mark used by permission of the British Toy and Hobby Association (BTHA); CE Symbol © European Union; Image of UKCA mark © Crown copyright. Contains public sector information licensed under the Open Government Licence v3.0; Dorling Kindersley/GI(X2); Lauren Shavell/GI; Science Photo Library/GI

Digital Quiz: BSI Kitemark logo is used with permission from the British Standards Institution; AlonzoDesign/GI

Key: GI = Getty Images

All information based on NHS print or online resources is correct at the time of publication.